MW01012793

RELAX AND SOLVE
CROSSWORDS

Publications International, Ltd.

Puzzle Creator: Harvey Estes
Images from Shutterstock.com

Brain Games is a registered trademark of Publications International, Ltd.

Louis Weber, CEO
Publications International, Ltd.
8140 Lehigh Avenue
Morton Grove, IL 60053

Permission is never granted for commercial purposes.

ISBN: 978-1-64558-406-3

Manufactured in China.

8 7 6 5 4 3 2 1

Let's get social!
@Publications_International
@PublicationsInternational
@BrainGames.TM
www.pilbooks.com

GIVE YOUR BRAIN A RELAXING WORKOUT

Great crossword puzzles should engage your mind while helping you unwind. That's what you'll find in *Brain Games® Relax and Solve: Crosswords.* We've assembled 84 crosswords that will keep your brain active while you decompress.

The puzzles may be difficult, but there are many ways in which you can solve these challenges. First of all, always work in pencil, because you never know when an answer you're "pretty" sure about ends up not fitting into the greater scheme of the puzzle. Also, always try to solve the fill-in-the-blank clues first; they are generally an easy access point into the more difficult sections of the puzzle. Other tips that may get your momentum going include trying to solve two- and three-letter, plural, and abbreviated clues first. These will hint at some of the longer, more difficult clues that you have not yet tackled. If you need a hint, check the puzzle key in the back of the book!

Whether you're a beginning puzzler or a seasoned pro, *Brain Games® Relax and Solve: Crosswords* contains something for everyone. You'll find 84 crossword puzzles with a variety of themes and levels of difficulty. So grab a pencil and get started!

ODE TO A GRECIAN-ERN

ACROSS

1. With 8-Across, a seabird abstaining?
7. Earth's lowest point
8. See 1-Across
9. With 11-Across, Swiss town of tough interrogation?
10. Got less intense
11. See 9-Across
15. Seeks in a dictionary, e.g.
18. Web-based business
21. Site for three men in a tub
22. With 23-Across, identification of trumpeter Laura?
23. See 22-Across
24. Secret romantic encounters

DOWN

1. Like "Romeo and Juliet"
2. Ash, for example
3. Out of control
4. Some apples
5. Changer of locks?
6. Gun or bayonet
7. Moral obligation
12. Glasses and such
13. Ready to go
14. V-8 ingredient
16. Drop in for a sec
17. Put in a good word for
19. Revival shouts
20. Golf course

Answers on page 172.

THE HALF MARATHON

ACROSS

1. Start of a quip about running a half-marathon
8. "Puh-lease!"
9. Painter Picasso
10. More of the quip
12. Hot spot
14. Win big, with "up"
16. More of the quip
18. One way to buy an item
21. "Good job!"
22. Cheat on
23. End of the quip

DOWN

1. ___ many words
2. The Gold Coast, today
3. Where drinks are on the host
4. Tall president, for short
5. Perform like Gregory Hines
6. It goes out on the beach
7. Carol, for example
11. "Madam Secretary" star Téa
12. Drink a bit
13. Wealthy contributor
15. IRA, e.g.
17. Slo-mo mammal
19. "Star Trek" genre
20. Bride's attire
22. Prefix with heel

Answers on page 172.

SELF-DESCRIPTIONS

ACROSS

1. Losing boxer's statement?
6. ___ polloi
8. Count with fangs
9. Pull some pranks
10. Make lasagna, e.g.
11. James Bond's cocktail
13. Revolutionary War firearm
15. Fly in the tropics
18. Ad infinitum
20. Major African artery
23. Court activity
24. Mascara site
25. "Sweet!"
26. Hurried person's statement?

DOWN

1. Race place
2. Town square
3. Island strings
4. "Good grief!"
5. Style of a room
6. Roster of enemies
7. Husband or wife's statement?
12. Singer Wagoner's statement?
14. Albatross, e.g.
16. With no ulterior motive
17. Financially strapped
19. Indian metropolis
21. Doesn't hold water
22. Get rid of

Answers on page 172.

WHERE TO?

ACROSS

1. Coleslaw source
8. Excited like Miss Piggy?
9. Top scout
10. Witty Coward
11. Dry red wine
13. Deodorant on a ball
14. Made cat sounds
17. Ship's servant
19. Well-traveled way
22. Military denial
23. Large lizards
24. Jazz singer/bandleader of the swing era

DOWN

1. "Suzanne" composer Leonard
2. "So what?!"
3. Central line
4. Inspire warm feelings about
5. First name in Christmas repentance
6. "Eat up!"
7. Group of five
12. Put your ears here
13. Not long past
15. "Another interruption?"
16. Bare-back rider?
18. No-frills
20. Not well-thought-out
21. Gasohol, for example

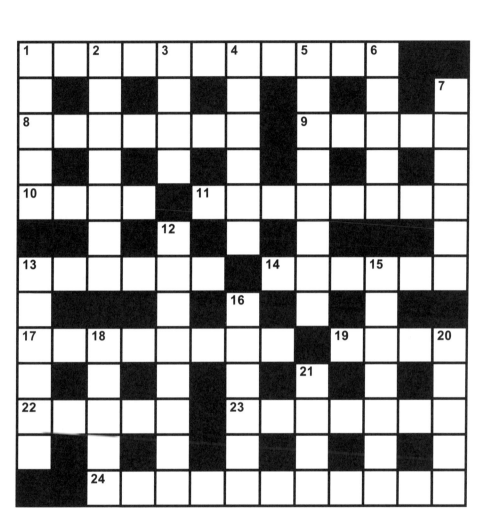

Answers on page 172.

ROLE REVERSAL

ACROSS

1. With 12-Across, appropriately named self-help book?
8. Wander around
9. Darken in the sunlight
10. "Ode to Joy" symphony number
11. Movie about Ruth
12. See 1-Across
17. Man bun, for one
19. Movie crowd member
21. Sixth sense
22. Misfit
24. Author of the self-help book?

DOWN

1. Available to rent
2. Island equivalent, to Donne
3. Got to
4. Took charge of
5. State, as a price
6. Weeping
7. Way of doing
11. Play the siren
13. Theoretically
14. Polar covers
15. Pass data along
16. Classified item
18. Ashley and Wynonna's mom
20. Steak order
23. Change color

Answers on page 173.

A FAMILY BUSINESS

ACROSS

1. Racer Donnie's brother
8. Church supper, maybe
9. What yes men do
10. Racer Ralph's son
12. Check time
14. Personal narrative
16. Racer Michael's father
19. Tex-Mex cause of heartburn
21. Wafer type
22. Racer Kyle's father

DOWN

1. Two-footer
2. One with a small part
3. "Tag! ___ it!"
4. LA team
5. Novel by Sir Walter Scott
6. Galley mover
7. Undiluted fruit juice
11. Boardinghouse sign
12. Spongy form of volcanic glass
13. Get rid of
15. "What an outrage!"
17. Incur, as debts
18. Pisa place
20. "Don't mind ___ do"

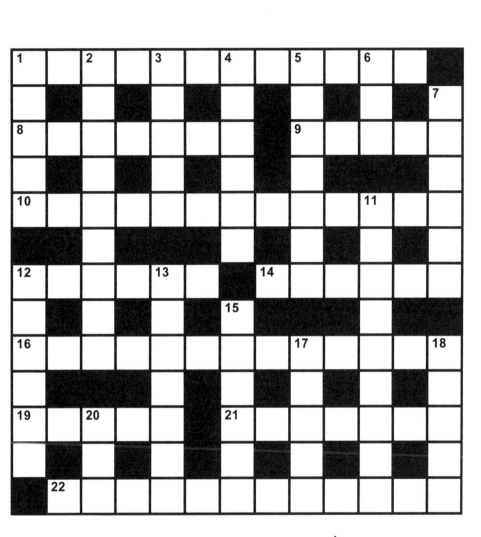

Answers on page 173.

TIE IT, YOU'LL LIKE IT

ACROSS

1. Understand how things are done
8. Org. for racial equality
9. Serenades
10. With 20-Across, use your influence
11. Type of bargain
13. Continuous
16. Tended the lawn
18. Stand-up kind of guy?
20. See 10-Across
22. "You'll regret that!"
23. Trifling to the max
24. "What pretty clothes!"

DOWN

1. Top dog
2. Words before fours
3. Prepare for printing
4. English derby town
5. Sty cry
6. Art stand
7. Blitzkrieg setting
12. Kind of insurance policy
14. Wandering
15. Pioneer in vaccination
17. Classified rectangles
18. Cruise ship accommodation
19. Political influence
21. Building location

Answers on page 173.

WHAT'S ON YOUR BED?

ACROSS

1. Featured article
8. Intercom system
9. Pro hoops org.
10. Took a catnap
11. Accepts reality
12. Euphemistic profanity
15. Dress in one's Sunday best
17. Geologist's hot stuff
19. The Get Up Kids' genre
20. Without thinking
22. It's lined with bars

DOWN

1. Nerve
2. Made a promise
3. Fly in the ointment
4. Vehicle with a meter
5. Orange leftovers
6. Kind of car lot
7. Hungarian composer Bela
11. Camera setting
12. Bell in a London clock tower
13. Kind of address
14. Cherubic, for example
16. Bathtime noise
17. Has the blahs
18. "You said a mouthful!"
21. Real suffix

Answers on page 173.

THEY CALLED MY NUMBER

ACROSS

1. With 9-Across, Cupid triumphed again?
5. "John B." of song
8. Racer Al or Al Jr.
9. See 1-Across
10. Hair-styling gadget
11. Like a seaman's humor
12. Overly sharp blade?
16. With 24-Across, carpet golf?
18. Tea type
21. "Don't bother explaining!"
22. Plain as day
23. Toy on a string
24. See 16-Across

DOWN

1. Make fun of
2. Drop by
3. Coup leader, perhaps
4. Drink without much alcohol
5. Bar orders
6. Shakespearean lady killer?
7. Beer bust, e.g.
13. Title for the Virgin Mary
14. Grandstander
15. Sirius, or Lassie
16. Suspicious
17. Follow, as orders
19. "You're ___ talk"
20. "She Loves You" refrain word

Answers on page 174.

VOICE VOTE

ACROSS

1. EYE
8. Park with animals
9. Nude evaluator
10. Launching of a rocket
12. Sudden thrust
13. NEIGH
17. Potato, for one
19. Like some returned goods
21. Playwright Levin
22. They were made for each other
24. ABS TENSION

DOWN

1. Eye color
2. Support with cheers
3. Boise's state
4. Play division
5. Hat attachment
6. Time and again
7. Game show host
11. Area of expertise
13. Nickname for a good kisser
14. Two-continent land mass
15. Lingerie item
16. First-born
18. "Well done!"
20. Do an impersonation of
23. "That's gross!"

Answers on page 174.

CLOSED-DOOR POLICY

ACROSS

1. Dressmakers' purchase, perhaps
8. Enter, in a way
9. Release
10. Stovetop vessel
12. Ruin the appearance of
13. Debate heatedly against
16. One who stays up late
18. It holds a little liquor
21. Close enough to hit
23. Had dinner at home
24. Epistle to be circulated

DOWN

1. To the point
2. Pretend to sing
3. Time after time
4. Music file holders
5. Picnics, and such
6. Sultan's palace area
7. Engine type
11. Don of game shows
13. Make a short visit
14. Shout of praise
15. Triumphant cry
17. Expressive, like a poem
19. Flip out
20. Sea salvage aid
22. Berliner's article

Answers on page 174.

GIVER OF GIFTS

ACROSS

1. With 10-Across, giver of gifts in winter
4. Suddenly be quiet
9. Something to jump for
10. See 1-Across
11. With 18-Across, giver of gifts in autumn
12. Green-eyed monster
14. Ambulate with attitude
16. Explodes
18. See 11-Across
20. With 24-Across, giver of gifts in the spring
22. "The Blue Danube," e.g.
23. Off base with permission
24. See 20-Across

DOWN

1. Tex-Mex treats
2. "No harm in asking"
3. Selected passage
5. Like a rainforest
6. Nostalgic souvenir
7. Annoyingly aggressive
8. Song for Scotto
13. Dirigible balloon
15. Go off on a tangent
16. Armed ship
17. "No kidding?"
18. Frequent chess sacrifice
19. Hummer's instrument
21. Diana's accessory

Answers on page 174.

WATERWAY TO GO!

ACROSS

1. Internet browser for waterways?
8. Interrogation room story
9. "Stop goofing off!"
10. Cop's cruiser
12. Serengeti grazer
13. Coats worn on waterways?
16. Pen contents
18. All tuckered out
20. Part of a football field
22. Title role for Valerie Harper
23. Prudence on waterways?

DOWN

1. Victory over all
2. Plane person
3. Capital near a game reserve
4. Kind of nut
5. Absolute, as nonsense
6. Thrown with force
7. Sci-fi weapons
11. Bourbon Street cuisine
13. Trembles with anticipation, perhaps
14. Do the jitterbug, for example
15. Place to find a stud
17. Comic strip named for a vine
18. Bunch of baby birds
19. Rough sketch
21. Marie Antoinette bathed in it

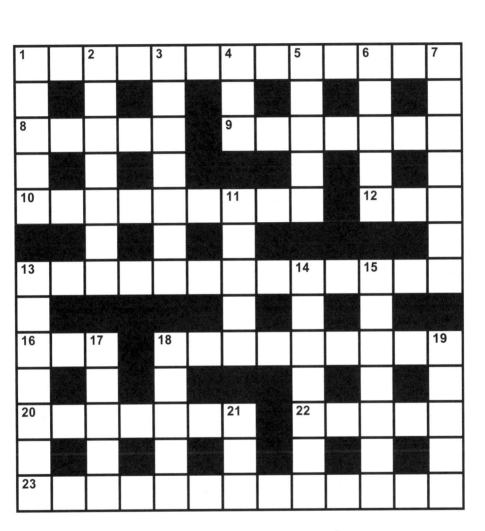

Answers on page 175.

WHAT LITTLE GIRLS ARE MADE OF?

ACROSS

1. Football event in New Orleans
8. "So, it's YOU!"
9. Apply primer, maybe
10. Change color
11. Add some excitement
14. Glossy finish
16. Takes care of
19. Part of a song title by Bryan Adams
22. Frequently, to a poet
23. Furnish food
24. Winter bug
25. Words said with a handshake

DOWN

1. "Don't leave me!"
2. Hula skirt material
3. Cold-blooded one
4. Martini garnishes
5. Tribute in song to "Mother Mary"
6. Make sense
7. Corp. honcho
12. Lunar-inspired Rodgers and Hart song
13. Oahu port
15. Tough one to sell
17. Cook in a wok
18. Gershwin's "I Got ___"
20. Luxury cruiser
21. Audacity

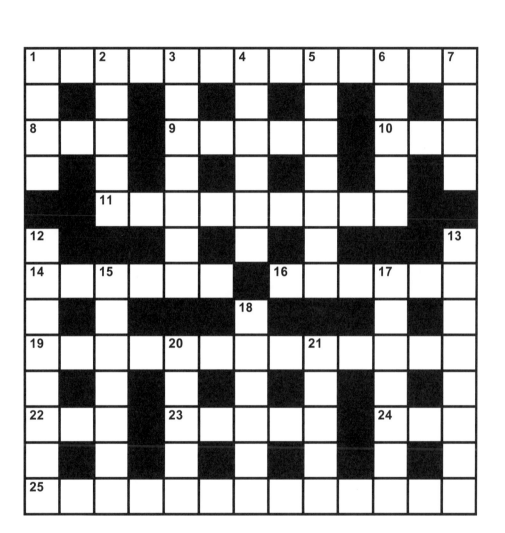

Answers on page 175.

IT'S A DOG'S LIFE

ACROSS

1. Free sniffers?
8. Wave makers
9. Brewski
10. Cheap guard dog?
11. "Good grief!"
13. Speaks pompously
16. Lap dog status?
20. Resolution time
21. Molar or bicuspid
22. Contemporary canine?

DOWN

1. Pull some pranks
2. "Like a Virgin" singer
3. Done too quickly
4. Youngster
5. Dresses to the nines
6. Closet pest
7. Gridiron officials
11. Rely
12. Work of 1606
14. Horse with a horn
15. Consecutively
17. Fruit with fuzz
18. Halved
19. Opposite of "in any way"

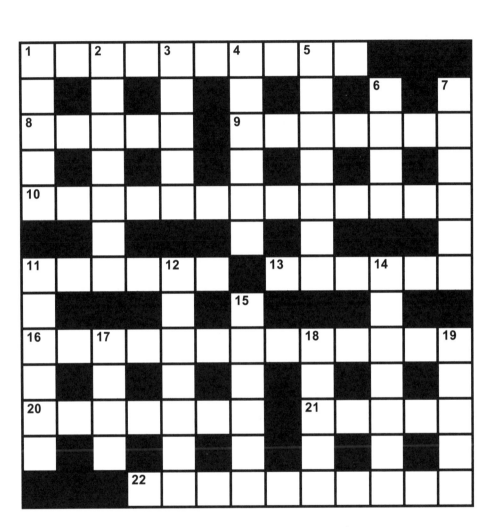

Answers on page 175.

33

THE NEW GEOMETRY

ACROSS

1. Appropriate approaches?
7. Just barely
8. Gives the thumbs-up to
10. Array of trucks?
13. In stock
14. He cometh on stage
17. Village eccentric?
21. Shoe spec
22. Dracula, for one
23. In favor of John Deere?

DOWN

1. Red stone
2. Aussie greeting
3. The old car, perhaps
4. Realm of C.S. Lewis
5. "Madam Secretary" star
6. "How should I know?"
9. Brew vessels
11. Bow and scrape
12. Made the scene
15. Like pottery
16. Tremble
18. Jerk
19. "See you later"
20. Hot tub features

Answers on page 175.

NAYSAYERS

ACROSS

1. Pickup basketball rule
9. Quick on the uptake
10. "The days just whiz by!"
11. Some kind of a nut
12. Start of a restaurant rule
14. More of the restaurant rule
16. Moaned and groaned
18. Intelligence agent
19. End of the restaurant rule
22. Engaged in hostilities
23. Pistol or saber
25. Weightlifter's rule

DOWN

2. Kind of nerve
3. Madonna's "Evita" costar
4. Short times
5. Clumsy lout
6. Editorial page material
7. Hungarian composer Franz
8. Sound of amazement
13. Building manager
14. Petty concern
15. Skeptical retort
17. "You wish!"
19. Vera on "Bates Motel"
20. Her name is Anthony
21. "If ___ Hammer"
24. Blues Brothers, e.g.

Answers on page 176.

CLOTHES-ING UP

ACROSS

1. P.O. concern.
8. Tribute in song to "Mother Mary"
9. First showing
10. "You there!"
11. Comfy spot
13. "Shut up!"
16. Cheese used in dressing
18. Baby bear
20. Banish to Siberia
21. "Seriously?"
22. Impulsive moves

DOWN

1. Nothing, in slang
2. Kind of theft
3. Like busy people
4. Ma'am to a lamb
5. "What's ___?" (line from Bugs)
6. Short in the back
7. Dilapidated dwelling
12. Refuse
13. Fast food staple
14 Long Island iced tea ingredient
15. Rises in profits, e.g.
17. Make changes to
18. Belief summary
19. Makes a mad dash
21. Media monitor, for short

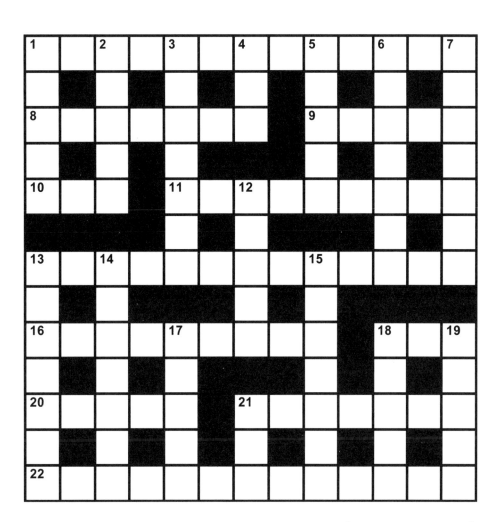

Answers on page 176.

PUTT'ER THERE

ACROSS

1. Intramural sport
8. Voyage of vanity?
9. Accepted doctrine
10. Controversial issue
12. You betcha
13. Global warming factor
16. The Greatest, in boxing
18. Texas border river
21. Dutch resort isle
22. Cloth by the sink
23. Tea party setting

DOWN

1. Blood partner
2. Peter or Paul, but not Mary
3. Movie title that's a state capital
4. Alley-___
5. Cool stuff, in slang
6. Like cancan dancers
7. "Dust in the Wind" band
11. '60s nightclub sign letters
13. "Get lost!"
14. Buddhist state
15. Lacking a brand name
17. Rodeo producer
19. Bob Marley, for one
20. All fired up
22. Woody, to Arlo

Answers on page 176.

SPREAD THE WORD

ACROSS

1. Featured article
8. Some Motown music, for short
9. Insomniac lack
10. Separated
12. Story on the stand
13. Polite substitute for swearing
16. Tangy pie flavor
18. "So talk!"
21. Humpty Dumpty as an intellectual?
23. Spot on a tie, say
24. Papers on a piano

DOWN

1. Cute hair features
2. Just ordinary
3. I, in a Will Smith movie
4. QB successes
5. Tart pie filling
6. Sandwich shop
7. Financial deficit
11. D.C. VIP
13. Ammo unit
14. Branagh of "Wild Wild West"
15. Like a good listener
17. Wise men
19. Altogether
20. Drink diluter, at times
22. Buck's partner

Answers on page 176.

43

SNOW PROBLEM, MAN!

ACROSS

1. 'S no pea
5. Get an eyeful
9. Specialized market
10. Forgo creature comforts
11. Source of sudden wealth
13. Blue shade
15. Baby bouncers
16. Model material
19. Drs.
21. 0, on a scoreboard
23. All fouled up
24. In isolation
25. Warm-hearted
26. 'S no bird, 's no plane

DOWN

1. Long and slender
2. Sonic boom speed
3. Last word
4. Cleverly skillful
6. Throbs
7. 'S no leopard
8. Head of a hive
12. Like some genes or jeans
14. 'S no cream
17. Extra space
18. Island of Japan
20. "Don Quixote" setting
22. Target for Dracula
24. Fearful reverence

Answers on page 177.

ALTERNATIVE ENERGY

ACROSS

1. Sailor's jacket
8. Summer refresher
9. Chef's wear
10. One you might not want to meet soon?
11. Overreacts, slangily
12. The three bears, for one
16. First phase
18. Animated musical of 1998
20. Long piano
21. Money for a taxi
22. Target of body blows

DOWN

1. Destroy completely
2. "That's a lie!"
3. Breath-taking snake
4. "Holy crow!"
5. Pakistani port
6. Extend "Time"
7. Hired guns
11. A Man Called ___
13. Pool sphere
14. Place for contributions
15. Doodle type?
16. Long tales
17. Select from the menu
19. Fibbers
21. Animation unit

Answers on page 177.

TRAFFIC LIGHT

ACROSS

1. Tend a tot
5. Yearns painfully
8. 1966 hit by The Cyrkle named for a sphere
9. Not soon enough
11. Roy Orbison's "Blue ___"
12. Georgia Tech athletes
15. Up to the time of
17. "That's true. However..."
20. Places to lie down in Psalm 23
22. Throwback style
23. Stud site

DOWN

1. Brimless hat
2. Cowpoke's sack
3. Hot spot
4. Big basin
5. Exercise method
6. "Stardust" composer Carmichael
7. Cardinals' home
10. Waiter's parting word after serving
12. Not so far along
13. Tony who sang with Dawn
14. Ban on trading
16. 140-character message
18. Reel person
19. "Here, try this"
21. Fearful reverence

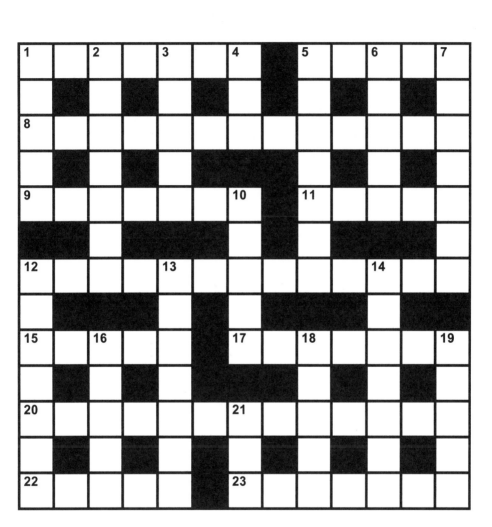

Answers on page 177.

CALL THE COPS

ACROSS

1. Neighborhood cop, e.g.
5. Some luxury cars
8. Hit the sack
9. Slangy way to say "No!"
10. Annoyed state
11. "I Remember You" band
12. Cop, as an authority figure
14. Cop of the highway patrol
17. Uninterpreted info
19. Bible book before Philemon
21. Royal domain
22. Cop who's a detective
23. Used pencils, perhaps
24. Time of low temps

DOWN

1. Get steamy
2. Refinish, perhaps
3. "Animal Farm," e.g.
4. Most peculiar
6. Major responsibility for a parent
7. Draw back
9. Going to the dogs, e.g.
12. Blush
13. Theft deterrent
15. Where meals are made
16. Fluorescent pigment brand
18. Humpback, e.g.
19. Like a wallflower
20. 4-0 World Series win, e.g.

Answers on page 177.

SHOW ME THE MONEY

ACROSS

1. Money, as a means to do something
7. "___luck!"
8. Humpty Dumpty as an intellectual?
10. Man changed in "A Christmas Carol"
11. " ___ Like It"
12. Tuxedo accessory
14. Sound of the wind
17. "Bald" flier
19. Add salt to a wound
22. Good shot
23. Hilariously funny incidents
24. Money, as an official medium of payment

DOWN

1. Princedom of Charles
2. Get taken down a notch
3. Muse of poets
4. "What an outrage!"
5. Nonsense
6. Feeling suspicious
9. High-carb word for money
12. Another high-carb word for money
13. Hazard in frozen waters
15. Unconscious
16. Baptism by fire
18. Elusive chalice
20. Enter uninvited, with 'in'
21. "Definitely not!"

Answers on page 178.

53

LOST IN THE MOVIES

ACROSS

1. Melville's whale hunter
4. Pressed for time
8. 2006 Leonardo DiCaprio film about a gem smuggler
9. Poe's "The ___ Heart"
10. Grown polliwog
11. PR agents concerns
14. Small shake
16. Lipinski leap
18. Flip out
21. 1995 Leonardo DiCaprio movie that is also a lunar event
22. Welcome gesture
23. X, on a greeting card

DOWN

2. Slice in two
3. Lead beside distilled waters?
4. Neighbor of Pakistan
5. Flowering shrubs
6. German sub
7. Bureaucratic excess
12. Fight with the fists
13. Academic type
15. Quick as lightning
17. Spill the beans
19. Bad habits
20. Watering hole

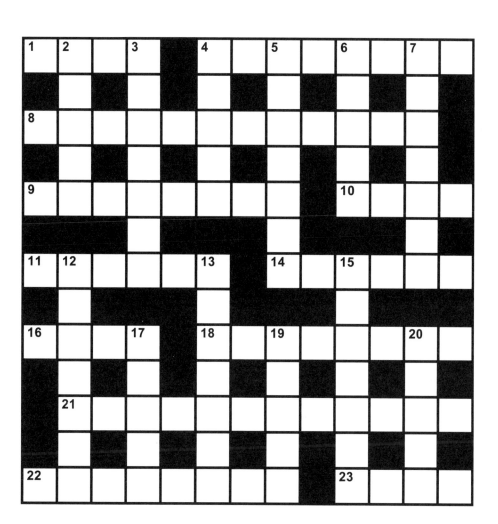

Answers on page 178.

55

PLAYING GOD

ACROSS

1. Religious comedy film of 2003
8. "Use it later" slip
9. Charlie Sheen, to Martin
10. "Wonder Woman" star Carter
11. Rudolph feature
12. He played the title role in 1-Across
16. Head honchos
18. Become narrower
20. Erode, with "away"
21. Actually
23. He played God in 1-Across

DOWN

1. More than just a pub regular
2. Strike-calling group
3. Cry out
4. Tell a tall tale
5. Like signed contracts
6. Class that dwells on the past
7. "Joltin' Joe" or "The Babe"
11. Travels aimlessly
12. It's between Mars and Saturn
13. Hustle and bustle
14. View a film online
15. Tot's art item
17. Séance board
19. Spectrum maker
22. Sports judge

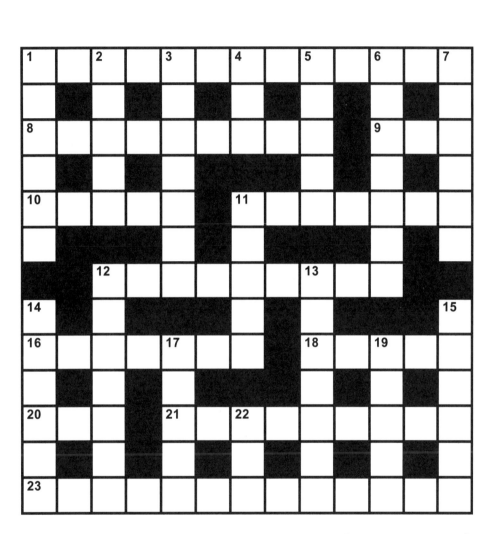

Answers on page 178.

WOMEN IN HIGH PLACES

ACROSS

8. First American woman in space
9. What borrowers do
10. Deep down
11. Complete mayhem
12. "Green" energy source
13. 8-Across, for example
15. 24-Across, for example
17. "Get off my property," in dog-speak
19. Boob tube
21. Road to conflict
23. A roadie carries it
24. First woman in space Tereshkova

DOWN

1. Academy bestowals
2. Entire crew
3. "Modelland" author Banks
4. Give a clue regarding
5. Extend a hand
6. Where couch potatoes are planted
7. Catches on
13. Like some parents
14. Baked with a cheese topping
15. A little shut-eye
16. Whenever you're ready
18. All gung ho
20. Wine tasters' tastes
22. Arena for axels

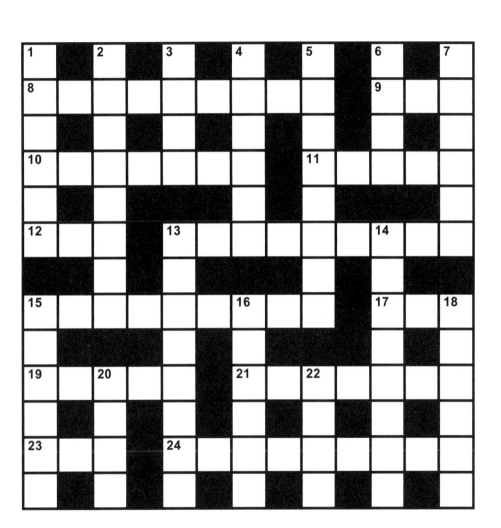

Answers on page 178.

SEE CRUISE

ACROSS

1. Tom Cruise title role of 1996
9. 31-day mo.
10. On edge
11. Toss of the dice
12. Mother lode
13. 1983 Tom Cruise where he danced in his skivvies
17. Get all decked out
19. Bran benefit
21. Starting today
23. Terrier's bark
24. 1999 Tom Cruise film with Nicole Kidman

DOWN

2. All fired up
3. Scenic transport
4. "Braveheart" star Gibson
5. Barely make it
6. "Just think!"
7. What's going on
8. Sunday speaker
12. Like cooked hot dogs
14. Initial phase
15. Little ones
16. Actor's reading material
17. "Platoon" Oscar nominee Willem
18. Bone connector
20. Linda Ronstadt's "Blue ___"
22. Become a better half

Answers on page 179.

JASON AND MELISSA

ACROSS

1. Movie with Jason Bateman and Melissa McCarthy
8. "Put a lid on it!"
9. "Amen to that!"
10. Plants in a dry place
11. Sci-fi weapons
12. Start of the movie's tagline
16. Diving suit hose
18. River traveler
20. Springtime prank victim
22. Blues Brothers, e.g.
23. End of the movie's tagline

DOWN

1. Crickets and beetles
2. Protestant work ___
3. Poke fun at
4. Athenian T
5. All choked up
6. Uncertain
7. Big celebrations
11. Variety show
13. Body part abused by rock bands
14. Tugs on fishing lines
15. Rundown shack, e.g.
16. "Cease!" on the seas
17. Domed home
19. Wheel spokes
21. ___Kosh B'Gosh (clothing brand)

Answers on page 179.

TV MOMS

ACROSS

1. Meredith Baxter played the mom for this show that debuted in 1982
9. Insignificant amount
10. Take out or in
11. Ram's partner
12. Yea-or-nay event
14. Florence Henderson played the mom for this show that debuted in 1969
18. With humility
20. Amenity in a resort
21. Burger or dog topper
22. Rake over the coals
23. Michael Learned played the mom for this show that debuted in 1971

DOWN

2. Discombobulate
3. Become frosted
4. Up to this point
5. Appearance, as in a mirror
6. Take a load off
7. Needing immediate attention
8. At liberty
13. "Gandhi" setting
15. Accept blame quietly
16. Prescribed inactivity
17. Filling and satisfying
18. Deposit with a pawnbroker
19. Born yesterday
20. Yogurt shop freebie
22. 1040 consultant (abbr.)

Answers on page 179.

ROCKET MAN

ACROSS

1. Author of the book that 14-Across is based on
5. The best pair in poker
8. Campers, for short
9. Per item cost
11. Vote for one not on the ballot
13. Florida metropolis
14. John Glenn was a character in this 1983 film
17. Awaiting a pitch
19. Laundry room vat
22. Election decider, perhaps
24. ATM access code
25. "Happy Days" extra
26. He played John Glenn in 14-Across

DOWN

1. Lose on purpose
2. It may be guided or heat-seeking
3. Good for something
4. G-man employer
6. Fine tableware
7. Old West lawman
10. Gasoline dispensers
12. Not at all
14. "All done!"
15. "Hello! I'm..." badge
16. In good condition
18. "I do" sayer
20. "Bye for now!"
21. Additional remuneration
23. Off the wall

Answers on page 179.

FBI MOST WANTED

ACROSS

1. Journalists, collectively
6. Place to dissect frogs
12. "Guitar Town" guitarist Steve
13. Baseball official
14. Easy as can be
15. Comics jungle queen
16. First person on the Most Wanted list (1950); shot to death his wife and her two brothers in 1949.
18. Group of very minor celebs
19. Belle's boyfriend
22. Rule of conduct
27. NBA and PGA, for two
29. Drop by on a whim
30. 1964 movie about a heist in an Istanbul museum
33. "Cool," to Ice-T
34. Allow to pass
36. The famed bank robber was #11 on the list (1950).
43. Handed out, as a citation
44. Big horned beast, briefly
45. California senator Feinstein
46. French film director Louis
47. Fancy house and grounds
48. Lawyers: Abbr.

DOWN

1. Bog moss
2. Aloe vera target
3. Cube creator Rubik
4. Dramatic basket
5. Flower part
6. Pres. before Clinton
7. Mummy in "The Mummy"
8. Audi rival
9. Perjured oneself
10. "Rule Britannia" composer
11. "String" veggie
17. Drink like a lady

19. Belfry resident
20. "___ Beso" ("That Kiss," Anka hit)
21. Cleo's cobra
23. "I understand" in radio lingo
24. N.T. book written by Paul
25. "Hairspray" actress Zadora
26. "Rizzoli & Isles" channel
28. Prominent, as a feature

31. Carolinas river
32. The "I" in TGIF
35. Myanmar's old name
36. Like a mason jar's mouth
37. Egyptian nature goddess
38. Atty.-to-be's exam
39. Beautiful moth
40. Pinball aborter
41. "We've ___ Just Begun" (1970 Carpenters song)
42. Con votes

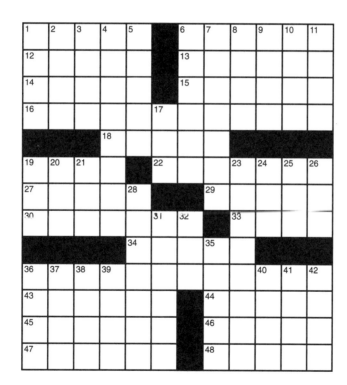

Answers on page 180.

CONSECUTIVE DEATHS

ACROSS

1. Dallas spinoff of the 1980s
8. Acorn or almond
9. Plugs and such
10. "Star Wars" series robot
11. Like most maps
12. With 14-Across, Los Angeles soap of the 1990s
14. See 12-Across
16. Clutter collector
18. High country
20. Diaper fastener
22. " ___ hear this!"
23. Hospital drama of the 2000s

DOWN

1. Royal realm
2. Accomplish more than
3. Some #@%*& individual
4. Work on a stage
5. Bamboozles
6. "Smells Like Teen Spirit" band
7. Yacht destination, maybe
11. Baby bird's noise
13. Friction match
14. Cartoon pig
15. Corrode or erode
16. Cuban coin
17. Fancy-schmancy
19. "Dueling" instrument
21. Black-eyed veggie

Answers on page 180.

HOLLYWOOD FEUD

ACROSS

1. Counterpart of Bette Davis in the FOX TV series "Feud"
8. Chompin' at the bit
9. Feathery accessory
10. "Hurray!"
11. Precarious position
12. 1981 biographical melodrama about 1-Across
15. Sailor
17. Worker with bricks
19. Feel sorry
20. Aggravated
22. She plays 1-Across in "Feud"

DOWN

1. Lewis or Seinfeld
2. Isaac's father
3. African region
4. Without further ___
5. Noted swing state
6. Bar mitzvah official
7. Confront the situation
11. Henry VIII's house
12. Big leagues
13. Crying
14. Beatles manager Brian
16. Thin pancake
17. Traveler's stop
18. Give an elbow
21. Female GI

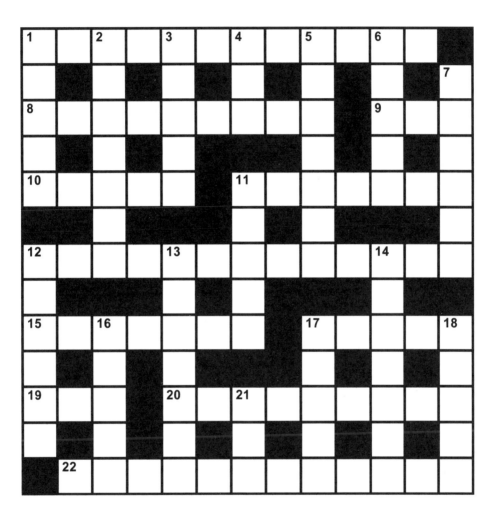

Answers on page 180.

BACK-TO-BACK VICTORIES

ACROSS

1. Doles out
8. Mind a youngster
9. Upright, for one
10. Alternative to pajamas
12. Be drowsy
14. "Emergency!"
16. "I give in!"
17. WWII president
19. Sniff out
20. Beat-up cars
23. "King Kong" star Watts
24. Tennis shots
25. They look at screens

DOWN

1. Arab emirate
2. Italian volcano
3. T-bill payout
4. Wine tastes
5. Post-season game
6. Kicks around
7. Handle difficulties
11. Do a great job
13. "Moby Dick" author
15. Exit
18. Face down temptation
19. What the Titanic did
21. Board chairs, e.g.
22. Capital of Ukraine
24. Letter repeated back-to-back in four answers

Answers on page 180.

TILL THERE WAS YOU

ACROSS

1. TILL
8. Fishing net
9. Way back when
10. With 19-Across, TILL
11. "Have a bite"
12. Stovetop whistler
14. Light lunches
18. Vacation lodgings
19. See 10-Across
22. Physically fit
23. Fabulous, to a theater critic
24. TILL

DOWN

1. Church supper, maybe
2. Illusory paintings
3. Unbelievable story
4. Tooth protector
5. Summer drink
6. Like a bad roof
7. Search, as for talent
13. Pays attention
15. Want so bad it hurts
16. Many a prime time series
17. Musical liability
18. Peculiar expression
20. Shape for some macaroni
21. Lacking clarity

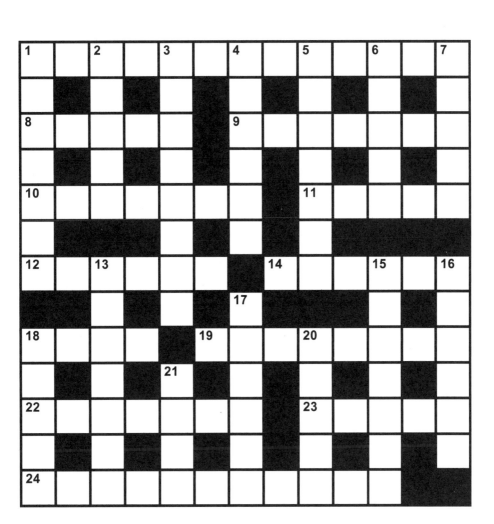

Answers on page 181.

THREE 45S

ACROSS

1. 45
8. Replay option
9. Mood music genre
10. With 14-Across, '45
11. Dry, as wine
12. Parting words
14. See 10-Across
17. Pro-prohibition
18. Baton-passing event
20. "Amen, brother!"
21. Map collection
23. .45

DOWN

1. Roast beef au ___
2. Like an open secret
3. Unauthorized DVD
4. Checked for fractures, perhaps
5. Smoldering fragment
6. Took care of
7. Private investigator
10. Class outing
13. Birds do it
15. Outfielder's catch
16. Health facility
18. Nostalgic fashion trend
19. Speak off the cuff
22. What to call an officer

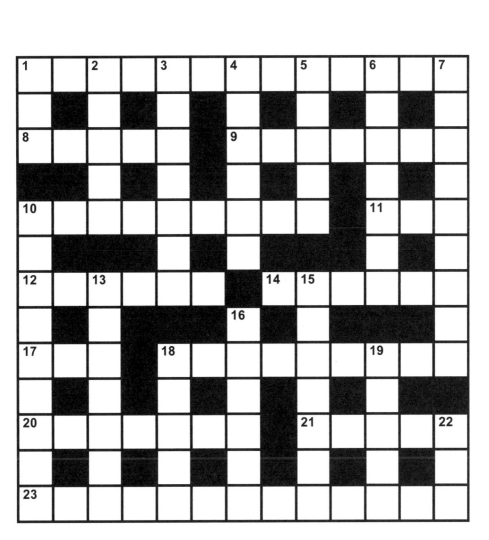

Answers on page 181.

GOING TOW TO TOE

ACROSS

1. The act of putting fruit in gin?
8. Like many a wrestler
9. Clean plate comment
10. Homes on wheels, for short
11. Not in the least difficult
13. Ride an iceberg?
16. Please the palate
19. Fanatic
21. In the zone
23. Repeated word in "The Trolley Song"
24. Hunger pang due to a piece of froot cereal?

DOWN

1. Fencing sword
2. Tended
3. "We'll see"
4. Earl Grey, e.g.
5. Taking time off
6. Daytime TV drama
7. All night flight
12. Brief disagreement
13. "Hit the road!"
14. 1979 Bette Midler film
15. Way back
17. One in a set of steps
18. Russian country house
20. Get dressed
22. London lavatory

Answers on page 181.

APPLE CORE

ACROSS

1. Loudly delicious
7. Ingredients for ice cream splits
8. "Outta sight!"
9. Court org.
10. Decisive
12. Lent prelude
17. Put up with
20. Scene of "Miss Saigon," briefly
21. Kind of bar
22. Place to secure a boat
23. Long isthmus divider

DOWN

1. Reach of the law
2. Sudden fright
3. Doubtfire's title
4. Horseman?
5. First words of "Satisfaction"
6. Oscar of "Sesame Street," e.g.
7. S&L, e.g.
11. Kind of whiskey
13. Seeing things as they are
14. Daytime timer
15. Consumes entirely
16. Pollution haze
18. Bean of old game shows
19. Render inaudible, with "out"
22. Word for apple at the center of 4 answers in this puzzle

Answers on page 181.

FOWL LANGUAGE

ACROSS

1. Doubletalk
8. Response to "You won't believe this!"
9. Seafood cookout
10. Intercom speaker
12. "Born In the ___"
13. Stand-up comedian Jeff
17. Hesitation sounds
18. Blockhead
20. Backyard basking spot
22. Footwear pair
23. Sheepless shepherdess

DOWN

2. "The joke's ___!"
3. Business, facetiously
4. Helper for Santa
5. Elizabeth I's favorite
6. Not clocked in
7. ATM feature
8. What to do
11. Halloween prop
13. Stocking style or angling device
14. Puts on the board
15. Evade, with "out of"
16. Dashes through the snow
18. Reside
19. "I give up!"
21. CIA counterpart

Answers on page 182.

SORRY

ACROSS

1. With 12-Across, "Sorry!"
5. Ticket remnant
8. Proportionately
9. Rock beater, in a game
10. Sit in on, as a class
12. See 1-Across
14. Bottom line
15. Sorry!
17. Home of the slender-waisted
18. Party manager, in Congress
21. With 24-Across, sorry
22. Vacation, for short
23. 140 characters or less
24. See 21-Across

DOWN

1. Weeping
2. Canon camera
3. You may get a rise out of it
4. Consume entirely
6. Pudding ingredient
7. Sound in a dog pound
9. "Saturday Night Live" bit
11. It vends odds and ends
13. Kids' jumping game
15. Employer's enticement
16. Chronic loser
17. Isle mentioned in "When I'm Sixty-Four"
19. Vietnam capital
20. Mild complaint

Answers on page 182.

87

AT'S SOMETHING ELSE

ACROSS

1. Your spouse's lawyer?
8. Agree to more issues
9. Small videorecorder
10. With 14-Across, NCOs getting hugs?
11. When tripled, a Beach Boys song
12. Places for mikes
14. See 10-Across
18. To boot
19. Blender beverage
21. Aces and eights, for example
22. Madonna musical
23. Halt like a streaker?

DOWN

1. Spray can
2. Piano adjuster
3. Unfair treatment
4. Luxury fur
5. Laura of "ER"
6. One hell of a guy?
7. John Lennon song about a lady
13. Gratis, to a lawyer
15. "That was easy"
16. Whole thing
17. Astronaut Buzz
18. "Swan Lake" attire
19. Orange Bowl site
20. Story on the stand

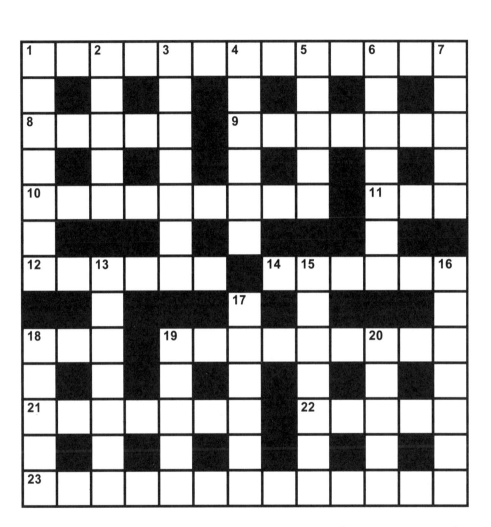

Answers on page 182.

ETHAN ALLEN'S DICTIONARY

ACROSS

1. Cantina order
4. With 8-Across, giving up just a little?
8. See 4-Across
10. Letters of debt
11. In shock
12. Eccentric sort
13. Cold spike
15. With 18-Across, elegant rensissance?
18. See 15-Across
21. Asimov's genre
23. "Fingers crossed!"
24. With 25-Across, on-topic animal keeper?
25. See 24-Across
26. Reply to roll call

DOWN

1. Stuck together
2. Whirlpool bath brand
3. Classic car
5. Tip over
6. "Open sesame!" sayer
7. Measure up to
9. Object of fan adoration
13. Reduced to rubble
14. Engineered simply
16. Choir platform
17. Allegedly harmful look
19. Nary a soul
20. Pub offering
22. PR concern

Answers on page 182.

WILD ANIMALS

ACROSS

1. Soothing, like ointment?
8. Unexpected defeat
9. Was taken down a peg
10. Way back when
11. Steakhouse selection
12. Prepare to dress for the forum?
16. Bochco legal drama
18. Not in custody
20. Press release
21. Awaiting a pitch
22. May registration?

DOWN

1. Semisoft cheese
2. "Don't worry about it"
3. Numerous, slangily
4. Completely confused
5. Highly skilled
6. Ship sunk at Pearl Harbor
7. Kind of crew
12. Deep ravines
13. Babe in a maternity ward
14. Off with permission
15. Crossed the threshold
17. About the moon
18. Ancient Mexican
19. Puzzle cube inventor

Answers on page 183.

HOW MUCH IS THERE?

ACROSS

1. Widespread panic
9. Hotel area
10. Barely used
11. Foreman's assistant
12. Room renter
13. With 20-Across, what you're good at
15. Figure enhancer
19. Bit of chill
20. See 13-Across
22. Kind of rap
23. Finals, for example
24. Decibel control

DOWN

2. Shady spot
3. Skeptic's comeback
4. Alert color
5. Movie shots
6. Get out of hand
7. City on the Nile
8. Yukon neighbor
14. You'd hear it in Toledo
16. Haifa inhabitant
17. "Despite all that..."
18. Bits of broccoli
19. Mideast desert region
20. English racing town
21. Hayes of "South Park"

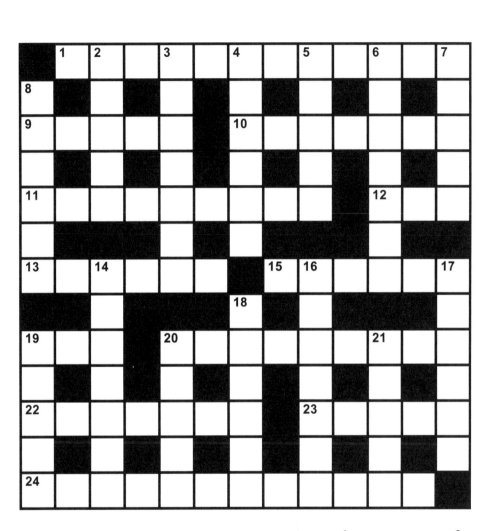

Answers on page 183.

GNOT IN MY DICTIONARY!

ACROSS

1. Fly flipper?
8. Age
9. Beyond the fringe
10. Contest venue
11. Some things disappear into it
12. Having a need to feed
14. Appropriate for everyone
17. Looks the other way
19. "We ___ please"
21. Dreamy fruit of Greek myth
22. In general
23. Antelope in a fraternity?

DOWN

2. Adjustable loop
3. Three of a kind beats it
4. News bulletin
5. Ashley and Wynonna's mom
6. Daily grind
7. City elf?
8. Town where they grind their teeth?
13. 24/7
15. "To Kill a Mockingbird" setting
16. Get away
18. Martini's partner in winemaking
20. Have a broken heart

Answers on page 183.

FAST FOOD, HASTY READING

ACROSS

1. With 9-Across, coin stamper?
5. Disney deer
8. Rack up
9. See 1-Across
10. With 18-Across, little white lie?
11. Maiden name preceder
13. Suffix with deposit or reposit
14. Having a tin ear
16. Dance under a bar
18. See 10-Across
21. With 24-Across, cowardly caretakers?
22. Defeated one's cry
23. Bloodhound's guide
24. See 21-Across

DOWN

1. Cotton on a stick
2. Place for a keystone
3. Trunk of Charles Atlas photos
4. Eagerly unwrap
5. More gloomy
6. Pietà figure
7. Where shekels are spent
12. Be successful in life
14. Car trunk item
15. Ladies' man
17. Pilgrim's corn
18. Sister of La Toya
19. When prompted
20. It's sometimes more

Answers on page 183.

YOU WANNA PIECE O' ME?

ACROSS

1. Blow up
9. Cups and saucers
10. Bug-eating plant
11. Listen
14. Stop fasting
15. Electronics whiz
17. Race to the _____
20. Gal's counterpart
21. Assist
23. Takes a closer look
25. Stale and then some
26. Tender help to a walker

DOWN

2. Hunter in the night sky
3. Historic period
4. Not in harmony
5. Energy beam
6. From the heart
7. Train station
8. Carve out of rock
12. Getting rid of
13. Title role for Valerie Harper
16. Give a false alarm
18. Lived off very little money
19. "Just the same..."
20. Thingamajig
22. Knot tying site
24. John or McCartney
25. Fireside chat pres.

Answers on page 184.

NCIS

ACROSS

1. Bridgelike game without bidding
6. Very commonplace
11. From that point on
12. "Fingers crossed!"
13. Mark Harmon plays this investigator on NCIS
15. Weather-vane turner
16. Inits. on a battleship
17. Cheese in a Greek salad
20. Crookshanks, in Harry Potter fiction
22. Hollywood legend Gardner
23. Superman accessory
27. Linda Hunt is ___ Lange on NCIS: Los Angeles
29. David McCallum is NCIS Medical Examiner Dr. Donald Mallard, nicknamed ___
30. Pass on the street
32. Carbon-14 determination
33. NY-to-Bermuda dir.
34. Leaky tire sound
35. Reactions to new babies
38. Ultimatum ender, often
40. Kensi Blye on NCIS: Los Angeles is played by ___
45. Emmy or Oscar
46. Planning to, informally
47. Wizards of old
48. Going overboard, for short

DOWN

1. Financial daily, briefly
2. Get a move on, quaintly
3. Savings acct. accrual
4. The "a" sound in "above"
5. "Desperate Housewives" actress Hatcher
6. 1999 Adam Sandler movie
7. Hawaiian tuna
8. De Niro's Manhattan restaurant
9. Alerts from the LAPD
10. "I took the one ___ traveled by": Frost
14. Start of a bedtime story

17. Late Saudi king
18. Till the cows come home
19. Jacques of "Mon Oncle"
21. Sch. of the Horned Frogs
23. Cereal grains in some bread
24. Berry at health food stores
25. UPS deliveries
26. Looks closely at
28. Sports bar screens
31. School starter

34. Salome danced for him
35. Eden evictee
36. Muted trumpet wail
37. Fishing line mishap
39. Starch from a tropical palm
41. Ticked-off feeling
42. Athlete's wear, for short
43. "Barbara ___" (Beach Boys classic)
44. "Macbeth" cauldron stirrer

Answers on page 184.

MARTIN SCORSESE MOVIES

ACROSS

1. Big bashes
6. CEO degrees
10. Woolly animal at a petting zoo
11. A psychic may see one
12. What the Sup. Court interprets
13. Eye part that contains color
14. 1990 De Niro gangster film directed by Martin Scorsese
16. Museum paintings
17. Filming location
20. Soap opera hunk, say
24. "How are you?" reply
26. Troop's camping place
27. 1975 De Niro film directed by Martin Scorsese
29. "To ___ own self be true": Shak.

30. Crime-solving Wolfe
31. Highwayman
33. Put in words
34. Buccaneer's bounty
36. 1980 De Niro film about a boxer, directed by Martin Scorsese
42. Plate with five sides
43. Carrie in "Carrie"
44. Manages, with "out"
45. Forearm bones
46. Isn't wrong?
47. Municipal maps

DOWN

1. Water cooler sound
2. "And another thing..."
3. Schifrin who wrote the "Mission: Impossible" theme
4. Brazilian novelist Jorge
5. Deemed appropriate
6. Performs halfheartedly, slangily

7. Balladeer Ives
8. "Elsa's Dream" is one
9. Backtalk
15. Young eel
17. Degree in letters
18. Beach at Normandy
19. Natural poison
21. Barry and Brubeck
22. "Aida" or "Tosca"
23. "Bad, Bad" Brown of song

25. Most considerate
28. NFL Hall of Famer Sanders
32. Gets dressed
35. Govt. note
36. Ostrich-like bird
37. Golf Hall of Famer Isao
38. Feds
39. Annapolis campus: Abbr.
40. Aspiring D.A.'s exam
41. Caustic soaps

Answers on page 184.

DAVID FINCHER MOVIES

ACROSS

1. Ripped, in gym lingo
5. "The ___ Network," 2010 film directed by David Fincher
11. eBay competitor
12. Bet to win and place
13. Sonic the Hedgehog company
14. Corroborate
15. Buckingham Palace monogram
16. Slangy greetings
17. Biblically yours
19. Banned chem. pollutant
22. Embroidery loop
24. Pepys work
26. Fully qualified
27. Macrame basic
28. Like people from Mecca
30. Diva's pride
31. A basketball, but not a football
32. Former French coin
34. Gobsmack
35. Disagreeably damp and chilly
38. Large unit of resistance
41. One may be swinging or sliding
42. Maple leaf, for Canada
43. Zip quantity
44. Like a pitcher's bag
45. "Ditto!"

DOWN

1. Australian wilderness
2. Car-ride company
3. 1999 Brad Pitt film directed by David Fincher
4. Agcy. that approves medicines
5. 1995 Brad Pitt film directed by David Fincher
6. Like Betty Boop
7. Sleepers and diners
8. French "here"

9. Org. that monitors gun sales
10. Put down, as linoleum
16. Perfect-game spoiler
18. Broke soil for planting
19. 2002 Jodie Foster thriller directed by David Fincher
20. Aussie water hazard
21. Eight bits in a computer
22. ___ doble (bullfight music)
23. Building beam
25. Byzantine image
29. Kind of logical statement
30. Family-size vehicle
33. Gin ___ (card game)
34. Arias for one
36. Top-notch
37. Small brown songbird
38. "La ___" (Debussy work)
39. Adjective for "pop punk"
40. "Pygmalion" monogram
41. Genetic fingerprint

Answers on page 184.

THREE BY BRADBURY

ACROSS

1. Be impolite at the table
5. Fem. title on a hacienda
8. "___, Our Help in Ages Past" (hymn)
12. Big name in spaghetti sauce
13. Early Air Force woman
14. Peru's capital
15. Very dry, as a desert
16. Like some dictionaries
18. 1957 Ray Bradbury novel
20. Brynner of "The King and I"
21. Missouri-to-Florida dir.
22. Nero's 401
25. Soft tennis shot
27. Daisylike fall flower
31. 1972 Bradbury fantasy novel
34. Soviet labor camp
35. Lumberjack's tool
36. Chicken ___ king
37. Hodges of the Dodgers
39. Air-pressure letters
41. 1983 Bradbury short story collection
48. Shake's cousin
49. Suburban burrower
50. Scott of "Hawaii Five-0"
51. Some NFL receivers
52. Big cheese at work
53. Acads. and univs.
54. Orbiting lab, for short
55. Restful resorts

DOWN

1. Diploma holder, briefly
2. ___ avis (uncommon find)
3. Opposed, in the sticks
4. Chum or pal
5. Accept, but maybe unhappily
6. Physics Nobelist Isidor
7. Jackson 5 hairdos
8. Cowboy's frontier land
9. Leslie Caron film of 1958
10. Forewarning, of a kind
11. Florida's Miami-___ County

17. Most crazy
19. One who makes passing remarks?
22. Bill amt.
23. Daddy's little girl: abbr.
24. Feeling poorly
26. Tony winner ___ Arthur
28. Refrain syllable
29. Snakelike fish
30. Actor Stephen of "Michael Collins"
32. Pacific atoll features

33. Making few stops, say
38. Christine of "Jack & Bobby"
40. Poetic feet
41. Mil. decorations
42. Colorful Apple model
43. Bible boatbuilder
44. Car turnarounds, slangily
45. In the ___ (informed)
46. Stylish Schiaparelli
47. Meeting of Cong.

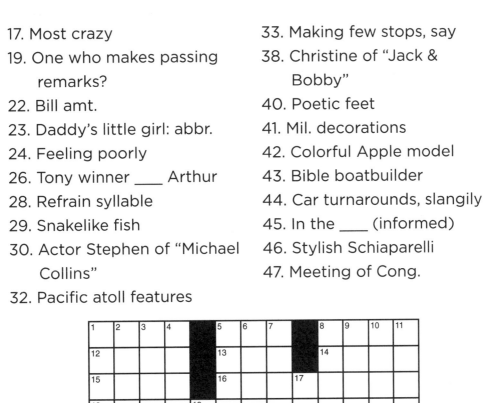

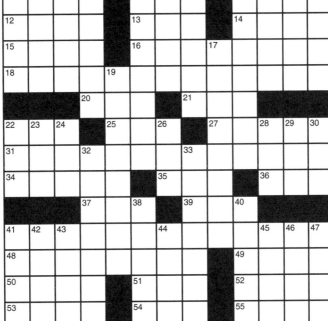

Answers on page 185.

109

THE UNABOMBER

ACROSS

1. Drink often served with sushi
5. Like most streets
11. Mongolia's ___ Bator
12. Balzac's first name
13. Four-sided fig.
14. Safer time to eat oysters, supposedly
15. Moroccan headwear
16. Shirts with pictures on them
17. Arab Spring country
19. Benchmark: Abbr.
22. Mount that Moses climbed
24. Kipling tiger ___ Khan
26. Bonnie belle
27. Egg-shaped
28. Good way to sing
30. Deplane dramatically
31. It comes between chi and omega
32. It merged with Mobil in 1999
34. Float gently in the air
35. Brief "despite"
38. Olympic skater Ito
41. Doc's prescriptions
42. Dead Sea artifact
43. It means "beyond"
44. Hippie-style pattern
45. "Green-eyed monster"

DOWN

1. Catch a wave
2. Out of the wind, at sea
3. The Unabomber was revealed to be former math teacher Ted ___
4. "The Lord of the Rings" tree creature
5. Babe Ruth's number
6. French's "The ___ Room"
7. Sean and Yoko
8. Came in first place
9. Getty Museum pieces
10. Casual "Sure"
16. "Didn't need to hear that!"
18. Move without effort

19. Number of years the Unabomber eluded authorities
20. Gillette ___ II razor
21. Bench press muscle, slangily
22. Chow for a sow
23. Authors Fleming and McEwan
25. Orange-roofed chain, familiarly
29. Like some checkups
30. Abbr. after a telephone no.
33. Case for Mulder and Scully
34. Authorities said Kaczynski's use of ___ seemed to be an obsession
36. Modern viewing option, for short
37. Anthem opener
38. Ariz. setting all year round
39. French for "here"
40. Beats By Dr. ___
41. Bovary's brief title

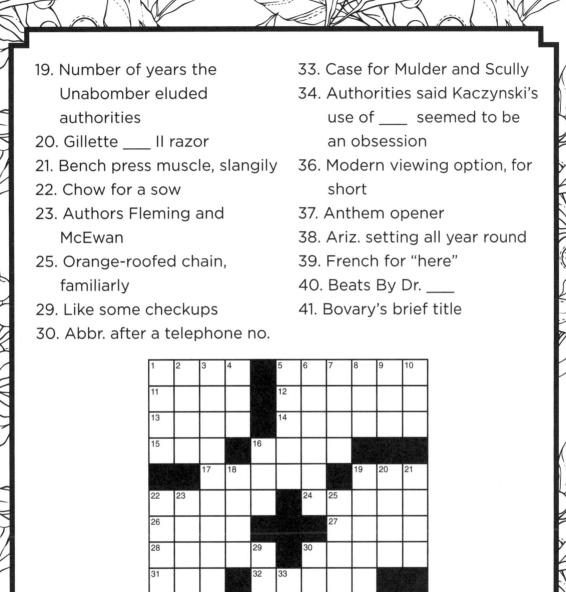

Answers on page 185.

TAKE A HIKE

ACROSS

1. Meals, to a lodger
6. Very cold
12. Friend of Kukla and Fran
13. Birthplace of Saint Francis
14. Historic Mississippi-to-Tennessee trail
16. Kind of beach breeze
17. Britain's health service: abbr.
18. Nonsense refrain syllable
19. Aladdin's magical pal
21. Spectacular trail along Australia's eastern seaboard
25. Arab rulers
26. Pea holder
27. Dept. that sponsors the 4-H club
28. Llama relatives
32. California trail along the Cascades and Sierra Nevada

35. Entertained
36. Famous woman of Troy
37. Renter, legally
38. Spanish islands

DOWN

1. Lead singer of U2
2. "The Good Earth" heroine
3. Space-bar bookends
4. Seismologist's scale
5. Makes less dangerous, as a bull
6. Give pause to
7. Queue after Q
8. Nat. that borders the Dead Sea
9. Designer Versace
10. Resort island off Naples
11. Trucker's fuel
15. He was, to Caesar
19. Small Italian dumplings
20. Stands the test of time
21. "Help me out here"

22. "Sure, why not?"
23. Traveling show
24. Huge, story-wise
28. ___ infra (see below)
29. Dickens's "Little" girl

30. On a voyage, say
31. RR stops
33. NASA's orbiting outpost
34. Lawyer's retainer

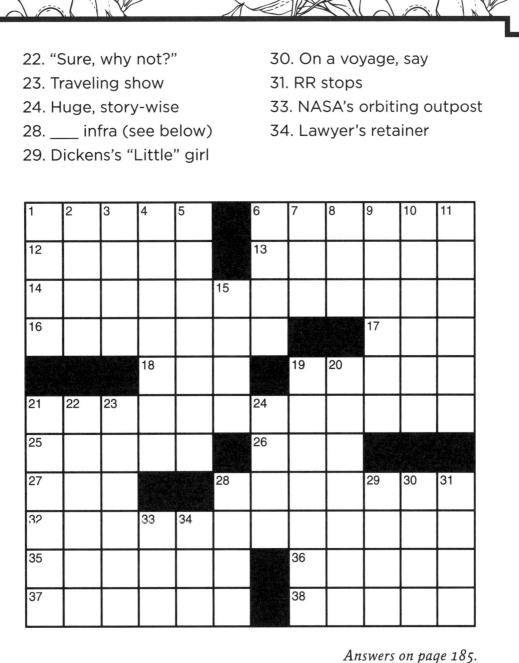

Answers on page 185.

WATERGATE

ACROSS

1. Breakfast drink
6. Building girder
11. Fur trader John Jacob
12. Beef casing
13. The threat of impeachment led to Nixon's ___
15. "One more thing"
16. Are, in the past
17. Physiques, informally
19. Society-column word
21. Charlottesville campus, for short
22. Nixon took steps to ___ the Watergate scandal
26. Release one's grip
28. Kin on mother's side
29. Five "burglars" were involved in the Watergate ___
31. The "p" of mph
32. "Read Across America" grp.
33. Cousin of "ahem"
34. Soothing lotion
37. Capricorn's animal
39. Washington Post reporters ___ and Carl Bernstein uncovered Watergate details
43. To the back
44. How losses are often shown
45. Emerald's mineral
46. Hairpin curves

DOWN

1. Bottle for pickles
2. Exhaust, with "up"
3. "See you then!"
4. Mattress springs
5. Energy units
6. Ore-___ Tater Tots
7. Betwixt and ___
8. Lake that sounds spooky
9. Bow-wielding deity
10. Hair on a lion's neck
14. Taboo to a toddler
17. Tulip-to-be

18. Eggs ___ easy
20. Tied, as a score
22. Popular pop
23. Jay-Z, LL Cool J and others
24. All-purpose trucks, informally
25. Chipper and frisky
27. Vessel's temporary bridge
30. "Aladdin" parrot

33. Chessboard sixteen
34. Common rhyme scheme
35. Body of tradition
36. Above, in Germany
38. "Garfield" beagle
40. The NBA's Magic on scoreboards
41. Mr. ___ (old detective game)
42. Dentist's deg.

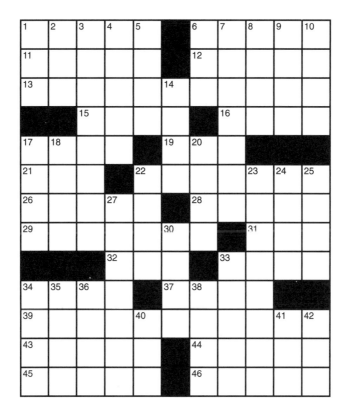

Answers on page 185.

STEINBECK CLASSICS

ACROSS

1. Farewell in old Rome
5. Colorado ski resort
10. Letter-shaped structural beam
11. Mail carrier's rounds
12. Steinbeck novel set in Monterey
14. Prepare to propose
15. Got down to Earth
16. Agcy. for entrepreneurs
18. "Eldorado" rock band
19. Steinbeck novel set in the Salinas Valley
23. Pub draft
24. One of the first TV superstations
25. Violas, cellos, etc.: abbr.
27. Clara Barton, notably
31. Steinbeck novel set on a ranch in northern California
33. Left, on a Spanish map
34. Affectedly precious, to Brits
35. Birth-related
36. Dates steadily

DOWN

1. Falcons quarterback Michael
2. Impose ____ on (outlaw)
3. Bowling alley section
4. Author Hemingway
5. Airport info next to "Dep."
6. Bean used to make miso
7. Inverted a stitch
8. Star, in France
9. Scientific Sir Isaac
13. Funny bone's joint
17. Bid ____ farewell
19. Sheena who sang "U Got the Look" with Prince
20. Gibson of tennis fame
21. Most parched
22. Blows, as a volcano

26. Madrid maiden: abbr.

28. Investment firm T. ___ Price

29. Blade in "The Mikado"

30. Peer group?

32. Conger, for one

1	2	3	4		5	6	7	8	9
10					11				
12				13					
14						15			
			16		17		18		
19	20	21				22			
23				24					
25			26		27		28	29	30
31				32					
33						34			
35						36			

Answers on page 186.

SAME CLUE

ACROSS

1. Candied tubers
5. View for an astronaut
10. Single item
11. Guardian Angels founder Curtis
12. BUCK
14. Former British prime minister
15. "Good Will Hunting" director Gus Van ___
16. Golfers' org.
18. Big T-shirt size: abbr.
19. BUCK
23. Card sent by a tchr.
24. K-O connector
25. Egyptian sun disk
27. Desert pit stops
31. BUCK
33. Calculus pioneer Leonhard
34. "Me also"
35. Rude look, sometimes
36. Camp shelter

DOWN

1. Southwest Arizona town
2. Med. school subject
3. Grain grinder
4. Prepares, as tea
5. Spanish "that"
6 Priests' robes
7. Crude or bawdy
8. Small, sharp pain
9. Tea-party host
13. Fit for royalty
17. Jousting wear
19. Carpentry and plumbing, e.g.
20. Choose not to participate
21. "A Streetcar Named Desire" shout
22. Soon
26. Brewer or Cub, for short
28. Locale, as on the Web
29. Musk of Tesla
30. One-armed bandit, briefly
32. "We ___ the World": 1985 Grammy winner

Answers on page 186.

MAKING A MURDERER

ACROSS

1. Supporting timber
6. Brew in a teapot
11. Happen
12. Buzzy abodes
13. Subject of Netflix true crime series
15. Bladed pole
16. Aviation: prefix
17. Narrow winning margin
18. Blasting inits.
21. Dances like Cinderella's
24. Bad place for a roller skate
26. Lincoln and Vigoda
27. "Grand Theft ___" (video game)
28. Continue, as a subscription
30. Surprise win
31. Little green men, for short
32. Sooners' st.
34. Halloween shouts
35. Dish from taro root

38. Forensic evidence found in a car
42. Phobias
43. Give the boot
44. Like an area filled with fronds
45. Witherspoon of "Legally Blonde"

DOWN

1. "Believe" singer Groban
2. Prefix for eight
3. Big name in slushes
4. Soccer mom's vehicle
5. Radial patterns
6. Stock-market units
7. Record for later, in a way
8. First lady
9. Bard's "ever"
10. "Gangnam Style" performer
14. Photo orig.
17. Otherwise

18. Cross-shaped letters
19. Dark time, in ads
20. Bouncy pace
21. Like a fairy-tale cupboard
22. Act as lookout, say
23. Eyeglass part
25. Barcelona bar bite
29. Like pine scent, perhaps
30. Long, heavy overcoat
33. Bout stoppers, briefly

34. "___ in the U.S.A."
    (Springsteen hit)
35. King Cole's request
36. Wallet bills
37. Gilligan's spot
38. Closest pal, in text
39. "Life of Pi" director Ang
40. Kayaker's need
41. Bunyan's tool

Answers on page 186.

BERNIE MADOFF

ACROSS

1. Bakery come-on
6. "The ___ Mutiny" (Bogart film)
11. Armstrong of jazz
12. Speed up, in music: Abbr.
13. Madoff's "epic fraud" was a ___
15. Bailout computer key
16. Took a load off
17. Drink, for short
18. "Hollaback Girl" singer Gwen
20. Suffix for Nepal or Siam
21. Dishonest response
22. 2000 Oscar role for Julia
23. '60s TV horse
25. Batting nos.
26. Enjoy the library
27. Hindu title of respect
28. Ballpark figure, briefly
29. Regular haunt

33. Center of a simile
34. Foe of Frazier and Foreman
35. Neighbor of Neb.
36. The loss to many of Madoff's thousands of victims
39. Puts in the letter box
40. "Skyfall" singer
41. "I have left a legacy of ___," Madoff admitted to his victims
42. Not as high

DOWN

1. French peaks, to the French
2. Avian hangout
3. Part of a pound
4. "Les ___" (Broadway musical)
5. "Let me repeat..."
6. Cholla and saguaro
7. "Alas!" in Austria

8. Titanic sinker
9. Moriarty, to Holmes
10. Madoff was convicted of ___ federal felonies
14. All there upstairs
19. Cut and run
22. Federal judge Denny Chin called Madoff's crimes "extraordinarily ___"
23. Handel masterwork
24. Almond liqueur
25. Airport listing
26. Kingly domains
27. Toni Morrison novel
29. Behind the times
30. "You didn't have to tell me"
31. Colonel insignia
32. Al or Bobby of racing
37. Boat-building wood
38. Affirmative at the altar

Answers on page 186.

123

SHUT DOWN

ACROSS

1. Biathlon need
6. Lily-like plant
11. CIA precursor
14. Bagel choice
15. Gazetteer data
16. Godfrey's instrument
17. Sign on a music school's locked door?
19. An Oscar statuette is mostly this
20. Handel oratorio king
21. Took turns
23. Weather map area
26. Rum and water make this
28. Is a gloomy Gus
29. Dish often served with hash browns
31. Low-scoring deadlock
33. Dwarf planet in the asteroid belt
34. Ringwald of "The Breakfast Club"
35. Org. providing jumps
38. Dummy's support
39. Nickel-copper alloy
40. Town, informally
41. Key near F1
42. On _____ (theoretically)
43. Kinshasa's river
44. _____ Tunes
46. Yucatán resort
47. Facetious nickname for a big guy
49. Satirical Mort
51. "Listen up!"
52. Serve-and-volleyer's strength, in tennis
54. Store window sign
56. Word to a doctor
57. Sign on a nuke plant's locked door?
62. Ill temper
63. IRA-enacting legislation
64. Expo '70 city
65. Some PD officers
66. Meal with the four questions
67. Chinese menu phrase

DOWN

1. Stick up
2. Suffix with serpent
3. Plywood source
4. Clark's love
5. Holds the attention of
6. "Little Iodine" creator Jimmy
7. Scepter's partner
8. Blackened tuna recipe word
9. Where to get a Volcano Double Beef Burrito
10. Increasingly rare table item
11. Sign on NASA's locked door?
12. Went downhill fast?
13. Enraptures
18. On the DL

22. Yahoo! competitor
23. John, "The Father of Liberalism"
24. Straws in the wind
25. Sign on a menswear store's locked door?
27. Albatrosses, as they're commonly known
30. Jeans brand
32. Card or D-back
34. Be a gloomy Gus
36. Plead one's case
37. Extreme suffering
39. End of an anniversary toast, perhaps
40. _____ mot
42. Thick soups
43. Pays a visit to
45. Web address ending
46. Spiced tea drink
47. Exemplar of slowness
48. Tin Woodsman's need
50. "_____ as I can throw him."
53. Geraint's woman
55. "Happy Motoring!" sloganeer
58. Suffix with Brooklyn
59. Seuss's Sam _____
60. Rubber-stamps
61. Pick, pick, pick

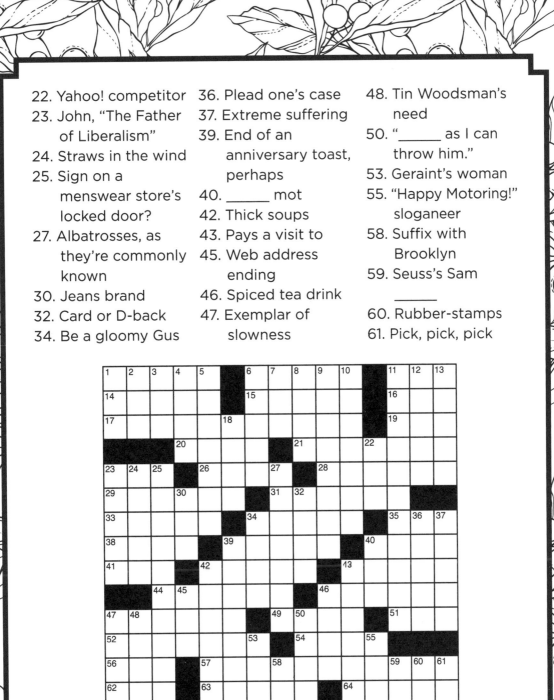

Answers on page 187.

HASHTAG HUMOR

ACROSS

1. Leftover bit of cloth
6. Golf-shoe gripper
11. "Star Trek" character with a Swahili last name
12. "Donnie ___" (1997 Depp/Pacino film)
13. Dutch colonists in South Africa
14. "___ Room": longtime kids' TV show
15. Hashtag for a movie about a prehistoric pig?
17. Hashtag for judges who are members of the bored?
18. Annoyance for a fairytale princess
21. "Didn't know that!"
22. "___ Kleine Nachtmusik" (classic Mozart piece)
25. Clear the chalkboard
27. Yeti and the Loch Ness monster, e.g.
28. Neighbor of 16-Down
29. A in French class
31. Cheer to a matador
32. Gives a hand at a card table
35. Hashtag for a rock star who has a crush on his guitar?
40. How an NBA game cannot end
41. Native American of Oklahoma
42. Is deserving of
43. Aired a second time
44. Gumby's pony
45. City, to Germans

DOWN

1. Predicate's partner: Abbr.
2. China's ___ En-lai
3. Regretful one
4. Lineup, as of troops
5. Section of a literary work
6. "Bad, Bad Leroy Brown" singer Jim ___

126

7. Eel-like fish
8. Phil in the Hockey Hall of Fame
9. Chromebook maker
10. Peter, eldest of the Monkees
12. Pickling liquid
16. Its cap. is Stockholm
18. Farm enclosure
19. Suffix with ranch or pistol
20. Termite predator
23. It awards the Stanley Cup
24. Point opposite WNW
26. Term of endearment
27. Heavenly streakers
29. "___ Gold" (1997 Peter Fonda film)
30. Abbr. on a returned check
33. "Jaws" island town
34. Beginning
35. Like a wet noodle
36. ___ cat (sandlot game)
37. Olympic swimmer with 12 medals ___ Torres
38. Brit's cry of astonishment
39. First-of-the-month payment

Answers on page 187.

JOHN GOTTI

ACROSS

1. Airport boarding area
5. One of Gotti's nicknames was "___ Don"
11. Difficult skating jump
12. Court crier's words
13. Get a new loan, slangily
14. Had a debate
15. Big initials in fashion
16. Annual stage award since 1956
17. "Good Vibrations" or "Surfin' Safari"
19. C.S.A. soldier
22. Assembly of church officials
24. Far from fresh
26. Final musical passage
27. As high as you can get
28. Tag ___ with (accompany)
30. Big name in cameras
31. Day of many a Fed. holiday
32. Familiar fruit logo

34. Aspersion
35. Golf peg
38. Obi Wan, to Luke
41. Breakfast or lunch
42. Nicholson's threesome
43. It's more, in a saying
44. Baby's knitwear
45. La ___ Tar Pits

DOWN

1. Cooper of "High Noon"
2. Cabin builders' need
3. After three acquittals, Gotti came to be known as the ___
4. Yale grad
5. Oil emirate Abu ___
6. Eagles' nests
7. Book leaf
8. Boston skyscraper, informally, with "the"
9. Daisy center
10. Crimson or scarlet
16. Curious

18. Advance from a shark
19. Capone, e.g., or Gotti
20. "Sesame Street" ticklee
21. Existed
22. A Ponzi scheme is one
23. Texter's "carpe diem"
25. Suspect's shadow
29. Aplenty
30. "All Things Considered" carrier

33. Change holder
34. Now, in the ICU
36. Comfortable situation
37. "Frozen" belle
38. Capo's crowd
39. "___ Beso" ("That Kiss," Anka hit)
40. Drill sgt. e.g.
41. Org. for the Boys of Summer

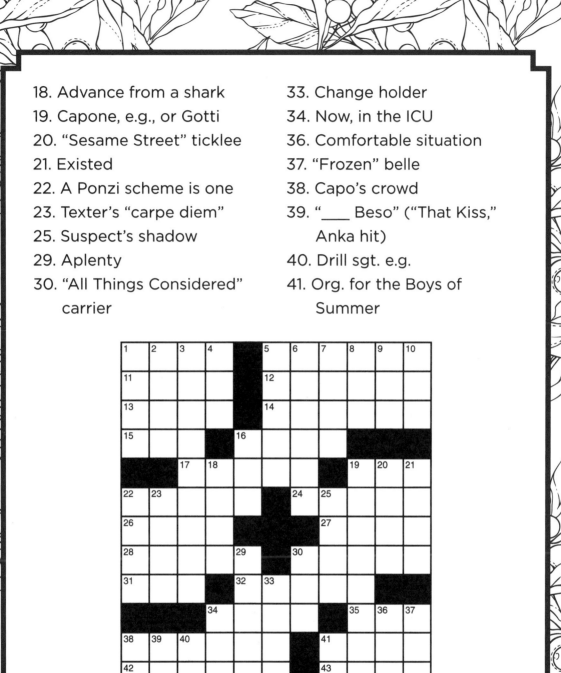

Answers on page 187.

LIFE IS BUT A DREAM

ACROSS

1. Ancient Greek square
6. High points
11. Biblical spy in Canaan (Numbers 14:36-38)
12. Opted
13. "Three Coins in the Fountain" fountain
14. "La Plume de Ma ___," 1958 Broadway hit
15. In his dream, who did Jacob see going up and down the ladder? (Genesis 28:12)
17. Singing satirist Tom
18. Antique sheen
21. Aug. setting in Atlanta
24. When he had his dream, Jacob slept on a ___ (Genesis 28:10-12)
27. CIO's labor mate
28. "Romanian Rhapsodies" composer Georges
29. The yellow Teletubby
32. Gideon's soldier dreamt of a cake of ___ overturning a Midianite tent (Judges 7:13)
37. Cheering deafeningly
38. Become used (to)
39. Bring delight to
40. "It's the ___" ("I had a makeover")
41. Cowboy's sport
42. "Thou shalt plant vineyards, and ___ them..." (Deuteronomy 28:39)

DOWN

1. Legal proceedings
2. Jake ___, first Congressman to fly in space
3. Cassini of fashion
4. Really relish
5. Chisholm Trail end
6. One pleased with long lines?

7. Make sore by rubbing

8. Pound residents

9. "___ Perpetua," Idaho's motto

10. "O ye ___ of Israel his servant..." (1 Chronicles 16:13)

16. Like a mannequin

18. O. T. book: Abbr.

19. Org. that hunts smugglers

20. Turnpike, for one

22. 'What's up, ___?"

23. Seesaw necessity

25. Needing assistance

26. Driver with a permit

30. Get ___ start (run behind)

31. Correo ___ (airmail): Sp.

32. 1930's boxing champ Max

33. "Alice's Restaurant" singer Guthrie

34. Dutch chess grandmaster Max

35. "For the ___ of the wicked shall be broken" (Psalms 37:13)

36. Almost-failing grades

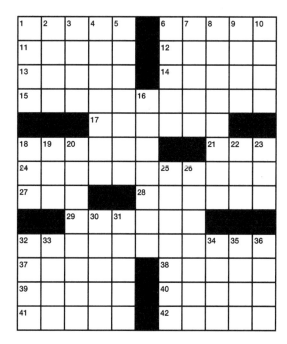

Answers on page 187.

PALINDROMES

ACROSS

1. Carpenter's tool, palindromically
6. Hyphen kin
12. "I Still See ___" ("Paint Your Wagon" tune)
13. Macho
14. Type of cabbage or a London hotel
15. Captivate
16. "Watch out for Fido and tabby!", palindromically
18. Like a runway model
19. "___ make a lovely corpse": Dickens
22. Arch or brew add-on
23. Genetic messengers
27. Middle: Comb. form
29. Traffic cone
30. Actress Remini of "The King of Queens"
31. "Mean Girls" actress Gasteyer, palindromically
33. 90-degree pipe joint
34. Revolted or rebelled

37. One North Pole notable visits Final Frontier org., palindromically
43. Country's boundary
44. Computer that weighed 30 tons
45. Smartphone feature
46. Utah mountain range
47. Problem for wooden ships
48. Chopper topper, palindromically

DOWN

1. "___ is more" (architectural principle)
2. Israeli resort city
3. Exhortation for le roi
4. Stock plans providing worker ownership: Abbr.
5. Time between flights
6. How to divide things to be fair
7. North Dakota's "Magic City"
8. Window treatments
9. Je t'___: I love you, in France
10. Vegas machine, for short

11. Belonging to that lady
17. Biblical father of Abner
19. Stomach acid, chemically
20. Like very wide shoes
21. Forensic material
24. N.Y. Mets' div.
25. "You've got mail" company
26. Tina Fey was its first female head writer, briefly
28. Oklahoma City's NBA team
29. Rabies vaccine developer Louis ___
31. Biblical landfall location

32. Destroyer that picked up an astronaut
35. Prefix meaning "wing" or "feather"
36. Morricone of film scores
37. Alphabet openers
38. Fly high, as an eagle
39. Its mascot is a mule
40. Isn't for some people?
41. Japanese P.M. who won the 1974 Peace Prize
42. Budget Rent-___

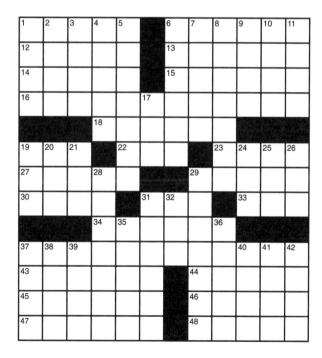

Answers on page 188.

SUMMER CAMPS

ACROSS

1. Outdoor jaunts at some camps
6. Some South Africans
11. Opted for
12. Figure skater Slutskaya
13. That one/this one/both
14. Sprites of Persian mythology
15. Aspirin tablet
17. First lady
18. "Enough is enough!"
22. "Buona ___" (Italian "Good evening")
23. Tasty treats at summer camp
27. "Kiss of the Spider Woman" star
29. Miss ___ of "Dallas"
30. Summer campers may see a lot of this
32. Overdue
33. Reacted in horror, say
35. "To Kill a Mockingbird" character

38. Hart's mate
39. Get on a soapbox
41. "The prettiest girl ___ saw..." (Start of "Sippin' Cider" camp song)
45. Allude (to)
46. Gemini rocket
47. Like a busybody
48. Vessel seen on many a camp lake

DOWN

1. Initials of fairy-tale author
2. Him, in Heidelberg
3. Decked in a boxing ring
4. Gullet
5. Opera ___ (opera buffa's counterpart)
6. Fun ride at some summer camps
7. British rocker Midge ___
8. Bygone Italian coins
9. Cambridge or Oxford, briefly
10. Self-addressed stamped env., for short

16. Mormon Church letters
18. Book identification no.
19. Aloe ___
20. The "E" in QED
21. NASCAR locale featured in a 2006 film
24. Chowder fish
25. High flier at some camps
26. Bird feeder tidbit
28. Outdoor activity at many a summer camp
31. Verdi aria "___ tu"
34. Ancestor of today's computers
35. Brought into the world
36. "Milk's Favorite Cookie"
37. Clumsy ones
40. Golf peg
42. Title akin to Rev.
43. "Microsoft sound" composer Brian ___
44. "Mittens" singer Carly ___ Jepsen

Answers on page 188.

BAKER STREET REVISITED

ACROSS

1. Chunk, as of concrete
5. Melodic motif
10. Word before Kitchen or Angels
12. Faced courageously
13. Of feathered friends
14. Not at all well
15. 1988 British comedy with Michael Caine as Sherlock
17. One way to be missed
18. At the stern
21. Brit's 26th letter
22. Done with
26. "The Woman," to Holmes
28. "West Side Story" girlfriend
29. Talkative bird
30. "Life of Pi" director Lee
32. Superb serve
33. Fable messages
36. 1979 "memoir" about adventures of Sherlock's brother, Mycroft Holmes
42. Major arteries
43. Airline seat choice
44. Agreement between nations
45. Blends or combines
46. Drawn-out battle
47. Place for a chin on a violin

DOWN

1. "Pygmalion" author
2. Big name in jeans
3. Got down from a horse
4. Down feeling, with "the"
5. Courtroom drama, e.g.
6. ___ days (happy time in the past)
7. Devil's specialty
8. Bill of fare
9. Jigsaw puzzle solver's starting point, often
11. Clock-radio button
12. With ___ breath (expectantly)
16. "If I Was" singer Midge
18. Align the crosshairs

19. Fish banquet
20. Gymnast's perfect score
23. By way of
24. List-ending abbr.
25. "Boy Problems" singer Carly ___ Jepsen
27. It may say "Hello"
28. Lustrous, poetically
30. Pretentious, as a film
31. "I'll have to pass"

34. Deliver a speech
35. More crafty
36. Diner sign
37. Edible seaweed used for sushi
38. Ancestry diagram
39. Getaway spot in the sea
40. Cutlass or 88, in the auto world
41. Chicks' hangout?

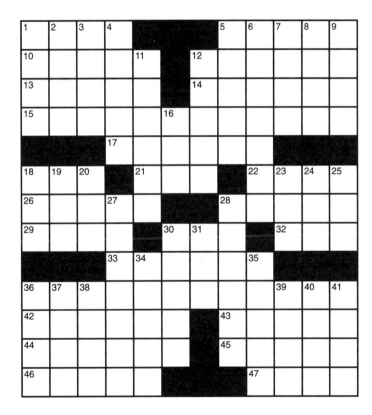

Answers on page 188.

BARBERSHOP QUARTET SONGS

ACROSS

1. Convent superior
7. Items on a to-do list
12. Caterpillars and such
13. Puts on the payroll
14. It's practically the national anthem of barbershop songs
16. Getting on in years
17. Muslim prayer leaders
18. Animal trap
19. A little gob
22. Thread weight, for silk, rayon, etc.
25. "____ I" ("Me, too")
26. 1931 tune covered by Sinatra, Dean Martin and many others
29. Does simple arithmetic
30. Pipe sections under a sink
31. Soap ingredient, once
32. Analyze the syntax of
34. "Fiddle-____!"
35. Buddy, briefly
38. Start of a 1931 Hoagy Carmichael song
42. "Great movie!"
43. Faithful wife of Greek legend
44. Persian sprites
45. Bowl or boat

DOWN

1. "And another thing…"
2. Cry like a baby
3. Brought up
4. Festive night, often
5. Imitation silk fabric
6. Beacon, e.g.
7. Kind of park or song
8. Feels below par
9. Mr., in Calcutta
10. Barbie's man
11. 180 from NNW
15. ____ es Salaam, Tanzania
18. Confession disclosures
19. Fluffy feathers

20. Adderall target, for short
21. All students at Eton
22. Call on a retro phone
23. Bathtub swirl, e.g.
24. Bump on a log
25. Popeye's ___' Pea
27. Ballet's Rudolf
28. Watch closely
32. Fuels from bogs

33. Ax-like tool
34. 552, in old Rome
35. Certain briefs, briefly
36. Descartes or Lacoste
37. Baseball's Hershiser
38. Abbr. on a pill bottle
39. Baseball's ___ Wee Reese
40. Atmosphere: Prefix
41. ___ in "Idaho"

Answers on page 188.

LARGE NUMBERS

ACROSS

1. Darns, say
6. Sound heard in jazz and rap
12. Completely crush, as a final
13. Vowel sextet
14. When you need to know what to call a ten followed by 39 zeros, here it is
16. Ballerinas
17. Engages in Halloween mischief, maybe
18. Island near St. Kitts
22. Basic card game
25. Chemist's place
27. Longest Swiss river
28. And if there are 42 zeros, it's this
31. Ford a shallow stream, say
32. Big letters in campgrounds
33. Its grads are lieuts.
34. Horoscope columnist Sydney
36. "All Things Considered" network

38. America's national bird
43. Now we're getting up there—63 zeros!
46. Group of nine
47. Antelope with spiral horns
48. Rudely awakens
49. Measures of force

DOWN

1. Grp. advocating tough liquor laws
2. Its cap. is Quito
3. Gas in some store signs
4. "Say that thou ___ forsake me..." (Shakespeare)
5. Often, a bell tower
6. Je ne ___ quoi (indefinable quality)
7. Beauty abducted by Paris
8. Engine leakage preventer
9. French for "king"
10. Yours, in Italy
11. "Atlas Shrugged" author Rand
15. "High Fidelity" star John

19. Big name in laptops and notebooks
20. Camaro muscle car
21. Capitol VIPS
22. Common tax form, spelled out
23. Composer Khachaturian
24. Hester Prynne's emblem
26. Eight-gold Olympic swimmer Matt
29. Headgear for Laurel and Hardy
30. Like most jackets
35. Charged toward
37. Pep ___ (morale booster)
39. Ford models of old
40. Composer ___-Carlo Menotti
41. Like Texas's star
42. Concludes
43. Part of KJV: Abbr.
44. Sea goddess who rescued Odysseus
45. Wildebeest's alias

Answers on page 189.

NEOLOGISMS

ACROSS

1. Color guard's holding
5. Salad-oil bottles
11. Do a stevedore's work
12. Apartment dweller, usually
13. Cyclotron particle
14. Cough medicine ingredient
15. By authority of
16. From way off
17. French military caps
19. Daisy ___ (Li'l Abner's love)
22. Desert rarity
24. Blue-winged ducks
26. Rhyme scheme of the "Rubaiyat"
27. Become unhinged
28. Ragout of roasted game
30. Having bulk and weight
31. Chicago-to-Atlanta dir.
32. Flapjack additive
34. Abbr. in some family businesses
35. Haul with great effort

38. Cajun's craft
41. Relax, with "up"
42. Japanese immigrant's grandchild
43. Richard who played "Jaws" in Bond movies
44. Chisholm Trail group
45. Comes to a finish

DOWN

1. Do a Chicken Dance move
2. Behind schedule
3. Neologism meaning socially inept but charming and cute
4. Emerald or sapphire
5. Neologism for a sci-fi movie about climate change
6. Holiday feast, e.g.
7. Exploitive one
8. "Exit full screen" key
9. Earl Grey or Darjeeling
10. Dry, on a wine label
16. Koko or Kong
18. Big cheese in Holland
19. Neologism for when a

guy "explains" something, condescendingly, to a woman

20. Cry said with a sigh
21. See at a distance
22. Backtalk
23. "Witness" actor Lukas
25. Biblical twin who sold his birthright
29. Jerusalem's country
30. Butterworth or Doubtfire

33. Neologism for opposite of a selfie—that is, a conventional photo of someone else
34. Cream of the crop
36. Like hand-me-downs
37. Gooey hair products
38. Science degree
39. Auto club inits.
40. Demolition letters
41. Just manage, with "out"

1	2	3	4		5	6	7	8	9	10
11					12					
13					14					
15				16						
		17	18					19	20	21
22	23					24	25			
26							27			
28				29		30				
31				32	33					
			34					35	36	37
38	39	40				41				
42						43				
44						45				

Answers on page 189.

RIDERS IN THE SKY

ACROSS

1. Tractor man John
6. Wide awake
11. Lineup of a sort
12. Muscle-bone connector
13. Celestial archer, usually shown as a centaur
15. Chastises
16. Word with guy or try
17. Get one's ducks in ___
19. Paste partner
20. Relative of khaki
23. Is sore
25. Sign of Aries
26. Alternative to Java or Python
28. Levin and Gershwin
30. Meeting to-do list
34. Pegasus, notably
36. Sherlock's lady friend
37. Gets stuck in mud
38. Coarse grass
39. French school

DOWN

1. Crow cousins
2. Spy novelist Ambler
3. Toy inventor Rubik
4. Sleeve type
5. Optometrist's application
6. Common baseball bat wood
7. Simba or Elsa
8. Make more rewarding
9. Save from danger
10. Messages with hashtags
14. British mil. medal
18. Pentagon simulation
20. Emergency situation
21. Capital of Zimbabwe
22. Pictured mentally
24. Man of the cloth
27. Chow down
29. Croon a tune
31. De ___ (Travis Bickle portrayer)
32. Fencing contest
33. Small African fox
35. Golf-ball prop

Answers on page 189.

SEEN AT PICNICS

ACROSS

1. Lab bottle
6. Give goosebumps to
11. '50s presidential hopeful Stevenson
12. D-day attack time
13. Beverage holder often seen at picnics
15. Ballpark fig.
16. "Othello" villain
17. 451, in old Rome
18. Indian lentil dish
21. Sultanate on Borneo
24. Desperate, as a situation
25. Grill area built in at some picnic spots
27. "The Mod Squad" character ___ Hayes
28. Desdemona's love, in opera
29. 60's antiwar grp.
30. Air Force hotshots
31. Fiber source in cereals
32. High-level U.S. award
35. Bug protector needed at many a picnic
39. "Okie From Muskogee" singer Haggard
40. Clubs for fairways
41. Hot coffee hazard
42. Baseball's Steady Eddie

DOWN

1. Disappear gradually
2. CEO and pres.
3. Came down, as onto a perch
4. "Do You Know the Way to ___ Jose"
5. "Don't Go Breaking My Heart" duettist, 1976
6. Japanese game akin to chess
7. Jimmy of shoes
8. Company founded by Steve Case
9. Deeply regret
10. Bungle the job
14. Colorful tabby that might

be seen at a Maryland picnic (it's a state symbol)
17. "Squawk Box" channel
18. Embassy VIP
19. Seed case
20. Jared in "Fight Club"
21. OPEC amounts, briefly
22. Brand of 35-Across, perhaps
23. Big coffee brewers
24. Actresses Sandra and Ruby

26. Item seen at any picnic
30. Curved like a rainbow
31. Boxing round ender
32. Bit in a bucket
33. Capital of Yemen
34. Classic computer game set on a seemingly deserted island
35. Chats with, online
36. IBM's Japanese competitor
37. Hacienda lady
38. Any NFL or MLB player

1	2	3	4	5		6	7	8	9	10
11						12				
13					14					
15					16					
			17					18	19	20
21	22	23					24			
25						26				
27					28					
29				30						
			31					32	33	34
35	36	37					38			
39						40				
41						42				

Answers on page 189.

SEEN AT THE GROCERY

ACROSS

1. Poultry for roasting spotted at grocery
5. Pancake topping from bees spotted at grocery
10. Blue-and-yellow megastore
11. Cole Porter's "___ We Fools?"
12. Long, slender loaf spotted at grocery
14. Litigious sorts
15. Words to a black sheep, in rhyme
17. Dollar in a jar, maybe
20. Colonial flagmaker
21. Herbal infusion tea
23. Clingy sandwich-covering product spotted at grocery
25. ___ d' (headwaiter)
26. Steak sauce brand spotted at grocery
27. Latv. or Lith., once
28. "Thank you," in Swahili
30. Slander counterpart
31. Pasta go-with spotted at grocery
37. Fenway Park team
38. Growth on a tree trunk
39. Typical Las Vegas gambler
40. Beanery sign

DOWN

1. "What's the ___?" ("Who cares?")
2. Kiev is its cap.
3. Ho-hum grade
4. School in Manhattan (but not in NY)
5. Like the Talmud
6. Bruin Bobby and family
7. Formerly known as, in maiden names
8. Spain's Victoria Eugenia, familiarly
9. Abbr. in a financial report
11. Cereal container spotted at grocery
13. Young scout
15. Ball-on-a-rope missiles

16. Light ___ (almost weightless)
17. Fortuneteller's deck
18. Beyond silly
19. Cartoon skunk Le Pew
20. Engine turns
22. Ballet about Princess Odette
24. Turncoat
29. DDE's rival

30. Do some high-tech surgery on
31. MTV show once hosted by Carson Daly
32. LBJ job-growth agency
33. Some 36-Down workers
34. Tony winner Merkel
35. Morris or Garfield
36. 24/7 service ctrs.

Answers on page 190.

AT THE PLAYGROUND

ACROSS

1. Playground teeter-totter
7. Spun platters, for short
11. American elk
12. Gernreich of fashion
13. Glitterati groups
14. Santa ___ (neighbor of Lompoc, California)
15. High-speed Olympic event
17. Glum
20. Israel's Meir
23. Blow up, as a photo: Abbr.
24. Important exam
26. Anti-drug org.
27. "Deep Space Nine" shape-shifter
28. The, in Italia
29. ___ Fields (mythical paradise)
31. Slangy affirmatives
32. Dislike to the max
33. Certain health plans
34. Silverware brand
37. Avoid deliberately

39. Horizontal-bar exercise at many playgrounds
43. Model's stance
44. Canada's largest department store chain until 1999
45. Act as an accessory
46. Playground "downhill" staples

DOWN

1. Flyer HQ'd in Dallas
2. Ending for ether or arbor
3. "Center" or "cycle" prefix
4. "Carrie" star Spacek
5. Alaskan island closer to Russia than to Alaska
6. Bit of smoke or hair
7. Wood deck trouble
8. Playground's climbing device
9. Netherlands city
10. Gillespie, to friends
16. Thomas Hardy's fictitious ___ Heath

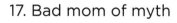

17. Bad mom of myth
18. Sixteen oz.
19. Structure at some playgrounds
21. "Seven Faces of ___" (1964 film)
22. A little fishy
24. Having a wavy pattern
25. "Sweet as apple cider" girl
30. Shakespearean poetic form

33. Dominican Republic neighbor
35. Chills champagne
36. Lentil-based dish (Var.)
37. Health resort
38. Play ___ with (make trouble for)
40. Auction gesture
41. A, in Avignon
42. Brief afterthoughts, in brief

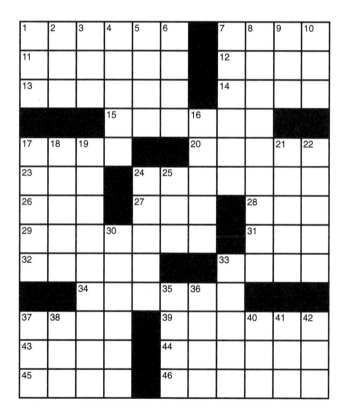

Answers on page 190.

CLIP JOINTS

ACROSS

1. Tusked porker
5. "Masterpiece Theatre" network
8. "Simpsons" bartender
11. Heraldic wreath
12. "Feels so good!"
13. Chow down
14. Name for a clip joint?
17. Diarist Nin
18. Congressional meeting: Abbr.
19. Corp. with a spinning globe and tower in its logo
21. Finnish steam bath
24. Part of a driver's exam
28. ___ ipsa loquitur (the thing speaks for itself)
29. Name for a clip joint?
32. Rain-___ (bubble gum brand)
33. Leave high and dry
34. Frame, in a bad way
37. Driver's 180
38. Aphrodite's son
40. Stallone's commando
44. Name for a clip joint?
47. Hindi "mister"
48. Composer Rorem
49. Abbr. on a building block
50. Entrepreneur's magazine
51. Dentist's deg.
52. Bad grades

DOWN

1. Florida beach city, informally
2. Straight ___ the rocks?
3. Gluck of the opera
4. Renaissance, literally
5. Rustic dads
6. Baffin and Chesapeake
7. Bowling rentals
8. Used a ruler
9. Blade for some boats
10. French for "summer"
15. Like a crookedly hung picture
16. Neighbor of Mex. and Can.
20. Agcy. concerned with work hazards

22. Emperor when Rome burned
23. PTA part: Abbr.
24. Flows back, as a tide
25. Christmas season
26. Not widely known
27. "Forbidden" fragrance
30. Mound of stones used as a marker
31. Worked, as clay or dough
35. Online address, for short
36. Hammer on
39. Defied radar
41. Store stock, briefly
42. Eight bits to computer folk
43. Ref. books sometimes sold with magnifying glasses
44. Forensics franchise
45. Big container for coffee
46. Commercial spots

1	2	3	4		5	6	7		8	9	10
11					12				13		
14				15				16			
17						18					
			19		20		21			22	23
24	25	26				27			28		
29							30	31			
32					33						
34			35	36		37					
		38			39		40		41	42	43
44	45				46						
47				48				49			
50				51				52			

Answers on page 190.

COLORFUL PHRASES

ACROSS

1. Easy wins
6. Hundred dollar bill, in older slang
11. Palm tree having betel nuts
12. "Based on ____ story"
13. Bulwer-Lytton's "It was a dark and stormy night...," e.g.
15. Diana Ross's group, with "The"
16. Grp. that now accepts girls
19. Afternoon brews
20. American Shakers founder
22. Turban-wearing believer
26. Babysitters, often
27. A bit spooky
28. Cast forth, as lava
29. When many duels were held
30. Stallion or stag
32. "____ for Noose" (Grafton book)
33. Long-neck clams

37. Inspector Clouseau movie, with "The"
41. Broadway investor
42. Greeting in Maui
43. Pied-a-____: part-time residence
44. At large

DOWN

1. Busta Rhymes's genre
2. Oklahoma sch. named for a televangelist
3. Mal de ____ (sea sickness)
4. HMO doctor designations
5. Military gestures
6. "It's A Wonderful Life" director Frank
7. Emphasized
8. Big date for a teen
9. "Great" river of England
10. Some tops
14. Fencing foil
16. Doesn't allow
17. "Just like that!" fingers sound

18. "Green Gables" girl
21. Member of Congress, say
23. Ayatollah's land
24. Big name in shoe polish
25. Chick tenders
27. Infinite
29. "Jacta est ___" ("The die is cast")
31. Capacious

33. Bit of a tiff
34. Fork prong
35. Bridge bldr.
36. Battle of Normandy town
38. Follower of boo or yoo
39. "How's that again?" syllables
40. "Norma ___," Field film

Answers on page 190.

THINGS YOU DO FOR LUCK

ACROSS

1. Twist master Checker
7. See 5-Down
12. Pointless, as an effort
13. Suffix with xeno- or techno-
14. Carousing
15. Sporty Camaros
16. Start of a cry from Juliet
18. Wear this for luck in Spain or China (but it must have been given to you as a gift)
24. Airport stop on New Jersey Transit, briefly
25. Class for US citizens-to-be
26. Fiorucci of fashion
27. "Rescue Me" star Denis
29. Excellent, slangily
30. Collector's suffix
31. There, in Latin
33. Coll. time period
34. Do this for luck in some countries
37. Japanese port near Nagasaki
38. Julia of "Julie & Julia"
41. Carry a foot from this for luck
45. "Should I risk it?"
46. Beverly who wrote "Dear Mr. Henshaw"
47. Writer ___ Boothe Luce
48. "Dallas" matriarch et al.

DOWN

1. Budget-managing exec
2. Attila for one
3. Acting guru Hagen
4. Elegant trinket
5. Kiss this (with 7-Across) for luck while hanging upside down, say the Irish
6. "My heavens!"
7. Secret observer
8. Pitcher
9. Tic-tac-toe triumph
10. "SNL" network
11. Some MIT grads
17. "Blazing Saddles" director Brooks

18. Ancient artifact
19. Panasonic accessory line with the slogan "Put some music on"
20. Brand for clearing a clogged pipe
21. "Fur ___" (Beethoven work)
22. Marksman, often
23. Boarding house sign
28. Hulk Hogan or Andre the Giant, slangily
29. Penny-arcade game
31. Partner of ands and buts

32. "Cobwebs From an Empty Skull" humorist
35. Hawkins of "Li'l Abner"
36. TV's "Lonesome George"
38. Agcy. promoting flu vaccines
39. "2001: A Space Odyssey" computer
40. Glass of "This American Life"
42. Chinese-born actress ___ Ling
43. Angry emotion
44. Baseball's Cobb and Hardin

Answers on page 191.

AESOP'S FABLES

ACROSS

1. Humped character in one Aesop fable
6. Bellow from Bossy
9. Chimp or orang
12. Amtrak's "bullet train"
13. Andean edible tuber
14. "Glee" actress Michele
15. Fable about a mouse with a great idea—but who will do it?
18. Bygone dagger
19. "Gross!"
20. Make a choice
23. Fleming and McKellen
25. DNA container
28. Character in four of Aesop's fables
30. Destiny
32. Donald Duck's nephews, e.g.
33. Mix, as cake batter
35. Approval vote
36. Knight's honorific
38. Like "Star Wars"
40. "Might makes right" is this fable's moral
46. Common Market inits., once
47. Reverent feeling
48. Diving duck
49. Character in two of Aesop's fables
50. Minor miscue on the court
51. Bogart's "Maltese Falcon" role

DOWN

1. Calloway who was in "The Blues Brothers"
2. Sleeve card?
3. Blanc of cartoon voices
4. 90-degree pipe bends
5. Kazan of "My Big Fat Greek Wedding"
6. ___ David (six-pointed star)
7. Calendar's 10th, briefly
8. "Hawaii Five-O" setting
9. Medieval quest for gold

10. "Once Upon a Mattress" veggie
11. Chow down
16. Comes closer
17. Coddled items
20. Frequently, in poetry
21. Golf-course standard
22. Divide into three parts
24. Flees (town)
26. Born, on society pages
27. H in Greek
29. Do drudgery
31. Van Gogh flowers

34. Guiding principle
37. Currency of Iran
39. Casino souvenir
40. Earl Grey, for one
41. "Little red" animal in a children's tale
42. Be in hock
43. Org. on a toothpaste box
44. Color of rubies and garnets
45. "I heard him exclaim ___ he drove…"

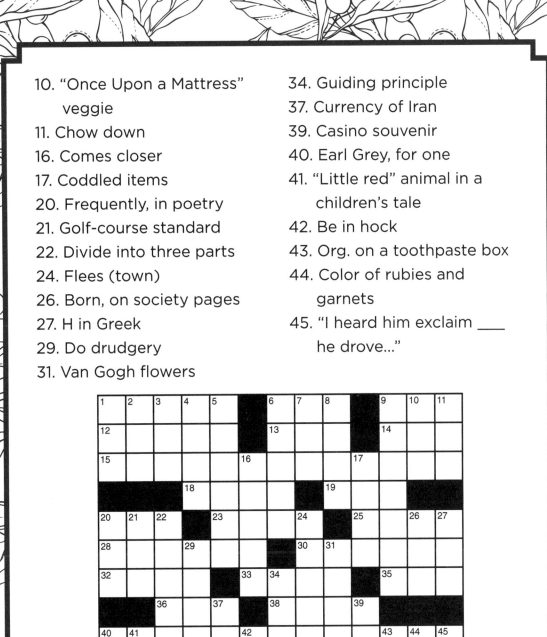

Answers on page 191.

WHAT'S IN A NAME

ACROSS

1. Blue stone
6. Pair with some pull
10. "Anna and the King" setting
14. Eye opener
15. Big fat mouth
16. Wrist-elbow connector
17. At the last second
19. Mastermind's scheme
20. Become upset
21. Where swimsuits may be worn
23. Dash types
24. Maryland player, for short
26. "Mother Night" author Vonnegut
27. Extreme deterrent
31. In jeopardy
34. Male sibs
35. _____ Lingus
36. Rosary component
37. "The Raven" poet
38. Concerning
39. Country est. in 1948
40. Florida city, informally
42. Man of the cloth
44. Coward's progenitor?
47. English channel, with "the"
48. Belted one out
49. Half a Latin dance
52. "Fess up!"
55. Churchill Downs area
57. Banjoist Scruggs
58. Athlete chauffeurs
60. Alan of "M*A*S*H"
61. Draft eligible
62. Beneficiary
63. Military meal hall
64. At no time, in verse
65. What the nose knows

DOWN

1. Jessica of "Blue Sky"
2. Mork, for one
3. Agreements
4. Ticks off
5. Sandpapers
6. Frisky swimmers
7. Onassis, to friends
8. Way up or down
9. Address
10. Crackerjack
11. Fidgety, e.g.
12. Quotation notation
13. Damon of "Green Zone"
18. Sideshow attraction
22. Dolls' friends
25. "Mosquito fleet" vessels
27. Spanish hero El _____
28. Red state

160

29. Reply to "Should we?"
30. Easy pace
31. Somewhat
32. TV host turned New Ager John _____
33. They're unique
37. Common desk items, briefly
38. Feel poorly
40. Jessica of "Seventh Heaven"
41. Traveling Wilburys member
42. Italian bridge
43. Concerns for
45. Beaux, informally
46. Petty concern
49. Dolly the sheep, for one
50. Virile types
51. Admirable quality
52. Clothes line
53. Under the weather
54. The sound of music
56. Univ. hotshot
59. Bee chaser?

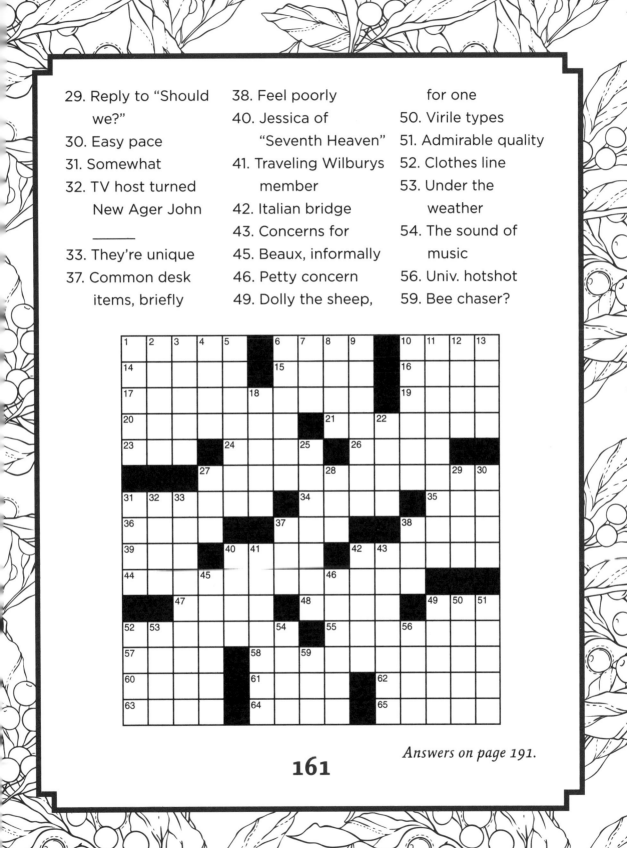

Answers on page 191.

LOTS OF S'S

ACROSS

1. Turn traitor
5. Police car sound
8. Op-ed piece, e.g.
9. Arc of many colors
10. Masters tournament city
11. Board for a seance
12. Source of salad leaves
15. Ancient African kingdom
17. Guest who forgot to cancel
20. Speed of sound
21. Acapulco pal
22. Having a twang
23. Vernal or autumnal occurrence

DOWN

1. "So long!"
2. Baked flatnoodles dish
3. "But of course!"
4. Pretend you don't notice
5. Leave secretly
6. Jewish scholar
7. Avant-garde
12. Word game with a stick figure
13. Doing great
14. Ideal, but impractical
16. Provides money for
18. Acronym for a big mess
19. Home team at Little Bighorn?

Answers on page 191.

163

COCKEYED OPTOMETRIST

ACROSS

1. Packs, for an explosion
6. Light regulator
11. Cable superstation
14. Have mercy on
15. Love, in the Louvre
16. Yes in Paris
17. "I pray for all"
19. Giant slugger
20. Woke up
21. Baked, in Bologna
23. Like the best food
26. On-the-go wedder
27. Court event
28. Herd, at times
29. Buttonhole
30. More sordid
32. Levels
33. "Optometrist," to 4 answers in this puzzle
35. Nice amount of moola: abbr.
38. Numberless groups
40. Right hand
41. Jeans type
43. Savages
45. They're Portuguese
46. Vituperates
48. Pub pals
49. Not troubled
50. Flying fig.
51. Ode for skinny rhymesters?
56. Singer Brenda
57. Tickle-me dolls
58. Fashion designer Perry
59. Hear here
60. Remote extents
61. Postpone

DOWN

1. Child's amt.
2. Visa statement abbr.
3. Half a cocktail?
4. General rule
5. Bagel choice
6. Illustrious
7. Whacked, old-style
8. Movie dog
9. Reveal
10. Herald
11. Licenses to play flutes?
12. Stick in the fridge
13. Indian lutes
18. Govt. agent
22. Behave like goop
23. Dry covering
24. Peace Prize city
25. Sweaty ceramics worker?
26. First name in humor
28. Needlefish
30. Bank deposit
31. It may be beaten
33. Development type

34. Proposal killers
36. Gray matter product
37. It may come before we forget
39. In plain sight
40. Sign of sanctity
41. That's a hot one

42. It's shaped like a trumpet
43. Measure of moonlight
44. Sounded like Harvey Fierstein
46. It can give you an edge

47. Houdini, at birth
49. "Don't look _____!"
52. Bullring "Bravo!"
53. Santa's helper
54. Even finish
55. Ukr., once

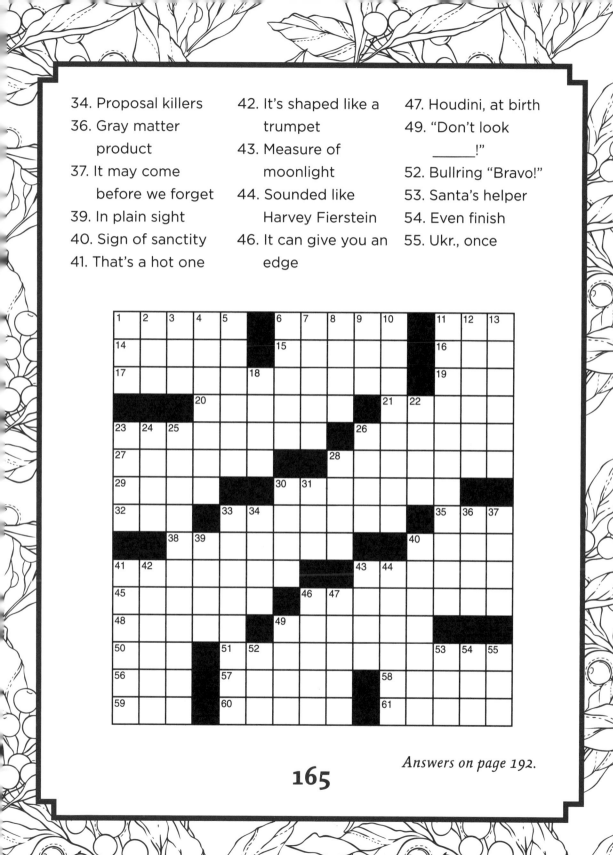

Answers on page 192.

NEGATIVE WORDS

ACROSS

1. Heart of the matter
5. Ill-equipped
10. "I put a spell ___..."
12. Disrepute
13. "The West Wing" creator Sorkin
14. Foals' mothers
15. One more than bi
16. A day in Spain?
18. Ben in the film "Ben"
19. Add salt and pepper
21. Be cheeky with
22. Strong dislike
24. Prefix meaning "wind"
25. Suffering 12-Across
29. Melancholy sound
30. Place to dip a quill
32. Sch. based in Ames
33. "Float like a butterfly" boxer
34. Tulsa coll. named for a televangelist
35. Fills up the truck

37. Implied but not stated
39. Confess (to)
40. Have ___ (talk)
41. Fishing mishaps
42. Anglo-Saxon worker

DOWN

1. Billies and nannies
2. How Alaska ranks No. 1
3. Damascus citizen
4. Besides
5. West Point initials
6. FDR home loan org.
7. Fawcett who played one of Charlie's Angels
8. "Whatever works"
9. Finals on campus
11. Downfall
17. Being threatened
20. Hidden stockpile
21. Wall Street purchase
23. Poisonous mushroom
25. Turn one's back on
26. Lizard kept as a pet
27. Eocene and Miocene, e.g.

28. Oscar Wilde's Gray
29. Farm storage buildings
31. "Cosi fan ___" (Mozart opera)

33. Pharaoh's serpents
36. Went after buried treasure
38. Card up the sleeve

Answers on page 192.

WORDS FROM OTHER LANGUAGES

ACROSS

1. From Inuit: Canoe-like craft
6. From Swedish, a bike with a small engine
11. Angler's basket
12. Brewmaster Coors
13. Ruben ___, Phillies Gold Glove-winning shortstop
14. Sophia Loren/Paul Newman comedy, 1965
15. Joplin forte
16. Abbr. for one with only two names
18. "Miracle on Ice" team
19. Regular beau
21. Online tech news site
22. From Arabic, plant with a heart?
24. Cager Olajuwon, in college
25. From French, courtship songs
29. Bell town in a Longfellow poem
30. Theme of noted King speech
32. Architect Mies van ___ Rohe
33. Actress Barbara ___ Geddes
34. "Girl on TV" pop band
35. Airplane without a pilot
37. Org. that hands out Oscars
39. Dark
40. Othello's people
41. From Czech, a Beer Barrel dance
42. From Spanish, backyard barbecue spot

DOWN

1. Dodge Aries and Plymouth Reliant
2. ___ di Mare (Italian clothing brand)
3. Chuck who broke the sound barrier
4. Atmospheric prefix
5. Gold rush region of 1897-98
6. Landlocked African nation
7. Harem chamber
8. Proverbial small town

9. French president's palace
10. Key of Debussy's "Clair de Lune"
17. Legendary capital of King Agamemnon
20. "Space Invaders" company
21. Naval rank below capt.
23. Miner's or caver's light generator
25. Camp-stove fuel
26. Garner who wrote "Misty"
27. Trap for congers
28. From Swahili, a hunting trek
29. Total, as a column of figures
31. Rapid, in music
33. Early software version
36. From Russian: Suffix with beat or neat
38. Bygone New Zealand bird

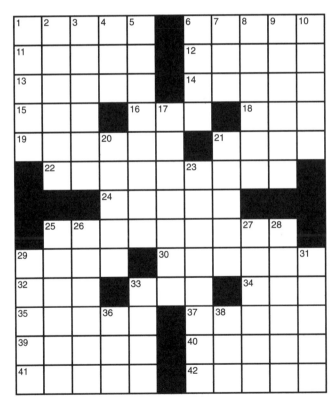

Answers on page 192.

AMERICAN PLAYWRIGHTS

ACROSS

1. Full of oomph
6. Big name in little trucks
11. Famous name on a plane
12. Gosling and Reynolds
13. "Who's Afraid of Virginia Woolf?" playwright
15. "Send a rescue ship!"
16. Home of the Burning Man festival: abbr.
17. Namibia, before 1990: abbr.
18. Caught congers
20. Caesar or tossed
23. "Deathtrap" playwright
27. All-___ (G-rated)
28. "Ditto"
29. "Glengarry Glen Ross" Pulitzer playwright
31. Big name in video chatting
32. Narrow strips of wood
34. "Guys and Dolls" playwright Burrows
37. Ling of "The Crow"
38. Apply lightly, with "on"

41. "To Kill A Mockingbird" screenplay writer
44. Mr. ___, bumbling cartoon character
45. Bird of prey's gripper
46. Bobsled turns
47. "The 39 ___," play based on a book and a Hitchcock film

DOWN

1. A lot of pizzazz?
2. ___-Chinese
3. Comic strip punches
4. Mao's group: abbr.
5. Spun, as a story
6. Commit a basketball infraction
7. Olive ___ (Popeye's lady)
8. Arrests, informally
9. Was aware of
10. Aboard a ship
14 Blue Hen state: abbr.
18. Artist's stand
19. Classroom fixtures

20. American playwright Shepard ("Buried Child")
21. The ___ Khan
22. Apollo 10's Snoopy, e.g., for short
24. "Oy ___!"
25. Dennis the Menace type
26. "Born," in wedding notices
30. Forbidden acts
31. Changes gears

33. "Saving Fish from Drowning" writer Amy
34. "Sigh!"
35. Givers of unfriendly hugs
36. Little units of work
38. "The Pineapple King"
39. At the crest of
40. Franklin and Bradlee
42. Baby's "piggy"
43. Bit for Mr. Ed

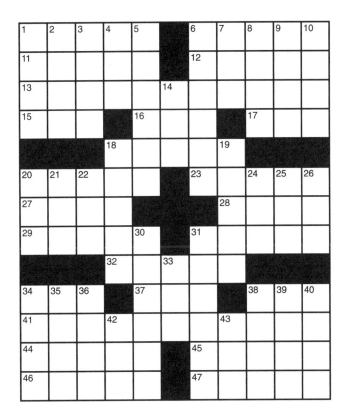

Answers on page 192.

ANSWERS

ODE TO A GRECIAN-ERN
(Pages 4-5)

```
    T E R N O F F T H E
    R   E   N   U   A   W
D E A D S E A   J U I C E
U   G   I   T   I   R   A
T H I R D   E A S E D U P
Y   C   U   A       Y   O
    D E G R E E B E R N
A   T           Y
L O O K S U P   E T A I L
L   M   A   L   W   M   I
S P A   Y O U R E D E R N
E   T   H   G   A   N   K
T O O T I N   T R Y S T S
```

THE HALF-MARATHON
(Pages 6-7)

```
    I M G O O D A T T H E
I   N   H   P   B   A   B   S
S P A R E M E   P A B L O   N
O   O   N   N       D   T   N
    C A R B O L O A D I N G
        A   E   N   D
I N F E R N O   C L E A N
M   A       N   E       E
B U T I S K I P   A S I S
I   C   L       G   C   T
B R A V O   T W O T I M E
E   T   T   A   W   F   G
        T H E R U N N I N G
```

SELF-DESCRIPTIONS
(Pages 8-9)

```
I M P O U N D E D   H O I
N   L   K   E   E   I   M
D R A C U L A   C U T U P
Y   Z   L   R   O   L   A
  B A K E   M A R T I N I
I   L   E       S   R
M U S K E T   T S E T S E
P   E       I   I       D
O N A N D O N   N I L E
R   B   E   D   C   E   S
T R I A L   E Y E L A S H
E   R   H   E   R   K   E
R A D   I M P R E S S E D
```

WHERE TO?
(Pages 10-11)

```
C A B B A G E H E A D
O   I   X   N   B   I   P
H O G W I L D   E A G L E
E   D   S   E   N   I   N
N O E L   C A B E R N E T
    A   C   R   Z       A
R O L L O N   M E O W E D
E       R   G   R   H
C A B I N B O Y   P A T H
E   A   C   D   F   T   A
N O S I R   I G U A N A S
T   I   I   V   E   O   T
    C A B C A L L O W A Y
```

172

ANSWERS

ROLE REVERSAL
(Pages 12-13)

```
V E N T R I L O Q U I S M
A   O   E E   U N     A
C O M E A N D G O   T A N
A   A   C     T   E   N
N I N T H   T H E B A B E
T   E   E   E   R   R
  F O R D U M M I E S
S   N     P   C   W
T O P K N O T   E X T R A
R   A   A   C   B   N
E S P   O D D M A N O U T
A   E   M   Y   P   N A
M O R T I M E R S N E R D
```

A FAMILY BUSINESS
(Pages 14-15)

```
B O B B Y A L L I S O N
I   I   O   A V   A   N
P O T L U C K   A G R E E
E   P   R   E   N       C
D A L E E A R N H A R D T
A       S   O       O   A
P A Y D A Y   M E M O I R
U   E   B   I       M
M A R I O A N D R E T T I
I   L   E   U       O   T
C H I L I   V A N I L L A
E   F   S   E   U   E   L
R I C H A R D P E T T Y
```

TIE IT, YOU'LL LIKE IT
(Pages 16-17)

```
K N O W T H E R O P E S
I   N   Y   P   I   A P
N A A C P   S I N G S T O
G   L   E   O   K   E L
P U L L S O M E   P L E A
I   E   U       N
N O N S T O P   M O W E D
O   A       B   A
C O M I C   S T R I N G S
A   A   L   T   E   T   I
B A D M O V E   L E A S T
I   I   U   U   L   D   E
N I C E T H R E A D S
```

WHAT'S ON YOUR BED?
(Pages 18-19)

```
  C O V E R S T O R Y
U   H O   U   A   I   B
S Q U A W K B O X   N B A
E   T   E       I   D   R
D O Z E D   F A C E S I T
    P       S   A       O
B L A N K E T Y B L A N K
I   E   O           N
G U S S Y U P   M A G M A
B   L   N       O   E   M
E M O   O N I M P U L S E
N   S   T   S   E   I   N
  S H E E T M U S I C
```

173

ANSWERS

THEY CALLED MY NUMBER
(Pages 20-21)

```
L O V E W O N ■ S L O O P
A ■ I ■ A ■ E ■ H ■ T ■ A
U N S E R ■ A N O T H E R
G ■ I ■ L ■ R ■ T ■ E ■ T
H O T C O M B ■ S A L T Y
A ■ ■ R ■ E ■ ■ L ■
T O O E D G E D S W O R D
■ ■ U ■ R ■ H ■ O
F O R E O N ■ O O L O N G
I ■ L ■ B ■ Y ■ W ■ N ■ S
S P A R E M E ■ O V E R T
H ■ D ■ Y ■ A ■ F ■ T ■ A
Y O Y O ■ T H E F L O O R
```

VOICE VOTE
(Pages 22-23)

```
H U R R I C A N E C O R E
A ■ O ■ D ■ C ■ A ■ F ■ M
Z O O ■ A R T C R I T I C
E ■ T ■ H ■ ■ F ■ E ■ E
L I F T O F F ■ L U N G E
■ O ■ ■ I ■ A ■
H O R S E R E S P O N S E
O ■ U ■ L ■ ■ I ■ L
T U B E R ■ D A M A G E D
L ■ R ■ A ■ I ■ H ■ E
I R A ■ S O U L M A T E S
P ■ V ■ I ■ G ■ I ■ I ■ T
S T O M A C H A C H E
```

CLOSED-DOOR POLICY
(Pages 24-25)

```
B O L T O F C L O T H
R ■ I ■ F ■ D ■ U ■ A ■ S
I N P U T ■ S E T F R E E
E ■ S ■ E ■ ■ I ■ E ■ A
F R Y I N G P A N ■ M A R
■ N ■ A ■ G ■ C
L O C K H O R N S W I T H
O ■ O ■ D ■ ■ M
O W L ■ S H O T G L A S S
K ■ Y ■ A ■ O ■ D ■ O
I N R A N G E ■ A T E I N
N ■ I ■ N ■ I ■ P ■ I ■ A
■ C H A I N L E T T E R
```

GIVER OF GIFTS
(Pages 26-27)

```
F A T H E R ■ C L A M U P
A ■ R ■ X ■ A ■ U ■ E ■ U
J O Y ■ C H R I S T M A S
I ■ M ■ E ■ I ■ H ■ E ■ H
T H E G R E A T ■ E N V Y
A ■ P ■ ■ Z ■ T
S T R U T ■ G O E S O F F
■ A ■ ■ U ■ P ■ O
P U M P K I N ■ P E T E R
A ■ B ■ A ■ B ■ E ■ I ■ R
W A L T Z ■ O N L E A V E
N ■ E ■ O ■ A ■ I ■ R ■ A
■ C O T T O N T A I L
```

ANSWERS

WATERWAY TO GO!
(Pages 28-29)

```
C H A N N E L S U R F E R
H V A   U T   L     A
A L I B I   G E T B U S Y
M   A   R     E N   G
P A T R O L C A R   G N U
  O   B     A       N
S T R A I T J A C K E T S
H     U       U   A
I N K   B O N E T I R E D
V   U   R       A L   R
E N D Z O N E   R H O D A
R   Z   O   A   U   B F
S O U N D J U D G M E N T
```

WHAT LITTLE GIRLS ARE MADE OF? (Pages 30-31)

```
S U G A R B O W L G A M E
T   R E   L   E D   X
A H A   P A I N T   D Y E
Y   S T V   I   U   C
    S P I C E I T U P   H
B   L   S   B       O
L U S T E R   S E E S T O
U   K     R       T   N
E V E R Y T H I N G I D O
M   P   A   Y   E R   L
O F T   C A T E R   F L U
O   I   H   H V   R   L
N I C E T O M E E T Y O U
```

IT'S A DOG'S LIFE
(Pages 32-33)

```
C O M P H O U N D S
U   A   A   R   M   Z
T I D E S   C O L D O N E
U   O   T   H   L   T   B
P E N N Y P I N S C H E R
E       N     N   U     A
D E A R M E   S P O U T S
E       A     I   N
P E K E C O N D I T I O N
E   I   B   A   N   C   O
N E W Y E A R   T O O T H
D   I   T   O   W   R   O
    C H O W F O R N O W
```

THE NEW GEOMETRY
(Pages 34-35)

```
R I G H T A N G L E S
U   D   R   A   E   E
B Y A H A I R   O K A Y S
Y   Y   D   N   N   R   T
      S E M I C I R C L E
K   S   I   A   H   I
O N H A N D   I C E M A N
W   O       Q   E   E   S
T O W N S Q U A R E
O   E   C   I   A   C   J
W I D T H   V A M P I R E
    U   M   E   I   A   T
P R O T R A C T O R S
```

175

ANSWERS

NAYSAYERS
(Pages 36-37)

```
N O H A R M N O F O U L
G   P   N   O   A P   I
A P T   T I M E F L I E S
S   I   O   E   N   Z
P E C A N   N O S H I R T
    I   T   U   O
N O S H O E S   P I N E D
A   A       E       R
S P Y   N O S E R V I C E
C   S   O   U   H   A
A T W A R   S I D E A R M
R   H   M   A   U   D O
  N O P A I N N O G A I N
```

CLOTHES-ING UP
(Pages 38-39)

```
Z I P C O D E N U M B E R
I   E   N W   P O   A
L E T I T B E   D E B U T
C   T   H   O   T   T
H E Y   E A S Y C H A I R
        G   A   I   A
B U T T O N Y O U R L I P
U   E       N   P
R O Q U E F O R T   C U B
G   U   M   U   R   O
E X I L E   F O R R E A L
R   L   N   C   N D   T
S N A P D E C I S I O N S
```

PUTT'ER THERE
(Pages 40-41)

```
F L A G F O O T B A L L
L   P A   O   A E     K
E G O T R I P   D O G M A
S   S   G   B   G     N
H O T P O T A T O   Y E S
    L   G   Y       A
G R E E N H O U S E G A S
O   I   G       E
A L I   R I O G R A N D E
W   S   V   A   E     A
A R U B A   D I S H R A G
Y   Z   N   A   T I   E
  C U P A N D S A U C E R
```

SPREAD THE WORD
(Pages 42-43)

```
C O V E R S T O R Y
U   A   O D   H D   R
R A N D B   S H U T E Y E
L   I   O     B   L   D
S P L I T U P   A L I B I
    L       O   R     N
B L A N K E T Y B L A N K
U   E       U     L
L E M O N   S P I L L I T
L   A   N       N E   O
E G G H E A D   S T A I N
I   T   O       U   R   I
  S H E E T M U S I C
```

ANSWERS

SNOW PROBLEM, MAN!
(Pages 44-45)

```
L I M A B E A N . G A W K
L A . A Y . D Q . C . . I
A N I C H E . R O U G H I T
K . H . O . E . E . . T .
. G O L D M I N E . S K Y
S . N . E . T . N . . C .
K N E E S . . B A L S A
I . . I . H . E . E . T .
M D S . G O O S E E G G
M . P . N . N . . R . V
I N A M E S S . A L O N E
L . I . R . H . W . O . I
K I N D . S U P E R M A N
```

ALTERNATIVE ENERGY
(Pages 46-47)

```
. W I N D B R E A K E R
H . R . O . O . G . A . E
I C E D T E A . A P R O N
T . C . T . . D . A . E
M A K E R . H A S A C O W
E . . . U . O . . . H
N U C L E A R F A M I L Y
. U . . S . L . . . A
S T E P O N E . M U L A N
A . B . R . . S . I . K
G R A N D . C A B F A R E
A . L . E . E . O . R . E
S O L A R P L E X U S
```

TRAFFIC LIGHT
(Pages 48-49)

```
B A B Y S I T . A C H E S
E . E . A . U . E . O . T
R E D R U B B E R B A L L
E . R . N . O . G . L . O
T O O L A T E . B A Y O U
. . L . N . I . . . L . I
Y E L L O W J A C K E T S
O . . R . O . . . M
U N T I L . Y E A H B U T
N . W . A . . C . A . A
G R E E N P A S T U R E S
E . E . D . W . O . G . T
R E T R O . E A R L O B E
```

CALL THE COPS
(Pages 50-51)

```
F L A T F O O T . B M W S
O . N . A . D . . . I . H
G O T O B E D . I X N A Y
U . I . L . E . D . O . A
P I Q U E . S K I D R O W
U . U . . . T . O . . . A
T H E M A N . S M O K E Y
U . . L . D . . . . . I
R A W D A T A . T I T U S
N . H . R . Y . I . C . W
R E A L M . G U M S H O E
E . L . . . I . E . E
D R E W . C O L D S N A P
```

ANSWERS

SHOW ME THE MONEY
(Pages 52-53)

```
W H E R E W I T H A L
A   A   R   N   O   E
L O T S A   E G G H E A D
E   C   T   V   W   R   O
S C R O O G E   A S Y O U
    O       R   S       G
B O W T I E   W H O O S H
R   C   O           U
E A G L E   R U B I T I N
A   R   B   D   A   C   O
D E A D E Y E   R I O T S
    I   R   A   G   L   I
  L E G A L T E N D E R
```

LOST IN THE MOVIES
(Pages 54-55)

```
A H A B   I N A H U R R Y
A   O   N   Z   B   E
B L O O D D I A M O N D
V   T   I   L   A   T
T E L L T A L E   T O A D
    E       A       P
I M A G E S   S H I V E R
I   C       N
A X E L   H A V E A C O W
I   E   O   I   W   A
T O T A L E C L I P S E
U   O   A   E   N   I
O P E N A R M S   K I S S
```

PLAYING GOD
(Pages 56-57)

```
B R U C E A L M I G H T Y
A   N   X   I   N   I   A
R A I N C H E C K   S O N
F   O   L   E   T   K
L Y N D A   R E D N O S E
Y   I   O       R       E
    J I M C A R R E Y
S   U   M   A       C
T O P D O G S   T A P E R
R   I   U   R   R   A
E A T   I N R E A L I T Y
A   E   J   E   C   S   O
M O R G A N F R E E M A N
```

WOMEN IN HIGH PLACES
(Pages 58-59)

```
O   A   T   H   R   S   G
S A L L Y R I D E   O W E
C   L   R   N   A   F   T
A T H E A R T   C H A O S
R   A       A   H       I
S U N   A S T R O N A U T
    D   D       U   U
C O S M O N A U T   G R R
A   P   T       R   A
T V S E T   W A R P A T H
N   I   I   I   I   T   R
A M P   V A L E N T I N A
P   S   E   L   K   N   H
```

178

ANSWERS

SEE CRUISE
(Pages 60-61)

```
J E R R Y M A G U I R E
P   A   A   E   E   M   V
A U G   I L L A T E A S E
S   E   L       B   G   N
T H R O W   P A Y D I R T
O   A       L       N
R I S K Y B U S I N E S S
    T   M   N       C
D R E S S U P   F I B E R
A   P   I   A   A   I
F R O M N O W O N   Y A P
O   N   E   E   T   O   T
E Y E S W I D E S H U T
```

JASON AND MELISSA
(Pages 62-63)

```
I D E N T I T Y T H I E F
N   T   O   A   E   N   E
S H H   Y O U S A I D I T
E   I   W       R   O   E
C A C T I   R A Y G U N S
T       T   E       B
S H E S H A V I N G T H E
    A       U   I       Y
A I R L I N E   B A R G E
V   D   G       B   A   S
A P R I L F O O L   D U O
S   U   O   S   E   I   R
T I M E O F H I S L I F E
```

TV MOMS
(Pages 64-65)

```
F A M I L Y T I E S
U   D   C   E   M   I   F
R E D C E N T   A L T E R
G   L   O       G   D   E
E W E   V O I C E V O T E
N       E   N       W
T H E B R A D Y B U N C H
    A       I   E       E
H A T I N H A N D   S P A
O   D   A       R   P   R
C H I L I   C H E W O U T
K   R   V   P   S   O   Y
    T H E W A L T O N S
```

ROCKET MAN
(Pages 66-67)

```
T O M W O L F E   A C E S
H   I   F   B       H   H
R V S   U N I T P R I C E
O   S   S       U   N   R
W R I T E I N   M I A M I
        L       O   P   F
T H E R I G H T S T U F F
H       D       O   P
A T B A T   W A S H T U B
T   R   A       E   O   O
S W I N G V O T E   P I N
I   D   D   Y       A   U
T E E N   E D H A R R I S
```

ANSWERS

FBI MOST WANTED
(Pages 68-69)

```
P R E S S █ B I O L A B
E A R L E █ U M P I R E
A S N A P █ S H E E N A
T H O M A S H O L D E N
█ █ █ D L I S T █ █ █
B E A U █ P R E C E P T
A S S N S █ █ P O P I N
T O P K A P I █ P H A T
█ █ L E T B Y █ █ █ █
W I L L I E S U T T O N
I S S U E D █ R H I N O
D I A N N E █ M A L L E
E S T A T E █ A T T Y S
```

CONSECUTIVE DEATHS
(Pages 70-71)

```
K N O T S L A N D I N G █
I U O C U I I
N U T A U T O P A R T S
G D N E V L
D R O I D T O S C A L E
O S W N
M E L R O S E P L A C E
U E E A
P A C K R A T T I B E T
E I I U A A
S A F E T Y P I N N O W
O E Z E I J A
█ G R E Y S A N A T O M Y
```

HOLLYWOOD FEUD
(Pages 72-73)

```
J O A N C R A W F O R D
E B O D L A F
R A R I N T O G O B O A
R A G R B C
Y A H O O T H I N I C E
A U D I
M O M M I E D E A R E S T
A N O P
J A C K T A R M A S O N
O R E O T U
R U E A T W I T S E N D
S P R A E I G
█ J E S S I C A L A N G E
```

BACK-TO-BACK VICTORIES
(Pages 74-75)

```
█ D I V V I E S U P █
A U E N I L C
B A B Y S I T P I A N O
U A U S Y P
S K I V V I E S D O Z E
E I X M F
S O S U N C L E F D R
T S E L E
S E E K F L I V V E R S
A P K I X I
N A O M I V O L L E Y S
K U E E L C T
█ T V V I E W E R S █
```

180

ANSWERS

TILL THERE WAS YOU
(Pages 76-77)

```
P L O W T H E F I E L D S
O P A N C E C
T R A W L A G E S A G O
L R L M D K U
U P T O T H E T R Y I T
C A L E
K E T T L E S A L A D S
U E T C I
I N N S T I M E T H A T
D E H N L E C
I N S H A P E B O F F O
O I Z A O O M
M O N E Y D R A W E R
```

THREE 45S
(Pages 78-79)

```
J U K E B O X R E C O R D
U N O R M V E
S L O M O A M B I E N T
W T Y E R E
F I N A L Y E A R S E C
I E D A T
E U L O G Y O F W W I I
L A C L V
D R Y R E L A Y R A C E
T E E I B D
R I G H T O N A T L A S
I G R I L I
P I S T O L C A L I B E R
```

GOING TOW TO TOE
(Pages 80-81)

```
S L O E M O T I O N
A V A E N S R
B E E F Y A L L G O N E
E R B F A D
R V S E A S Y A S P I E
A E V Y
G O W I T H T H E F L O E
E H T O
T A S T E G O O D N U T
L T R A G O
O N A R O L L C L A N G
S I S O H G U
T H R O E F O R A L O O P
```

APPLE CORE
(Pages 82-83)

```
L I P S M A C K I N G
O A R E C R
B A N A N A S N E A T O
A G I T N U
N B A C L I M A C T I C
K R R U H
M A R D I G R A S
U E S U S
S T O M A C H E D N A M
E R L R D O
S U S H I M O O R I N G
U O S A W A
P A N A M A C A N A L
```

181

ANSWERS

FOWL LANGUAGE
(Pages 84-85)

```
G O B B L E D E G O O K
  N   E   L S F     E
T R Y M E   F I S H F R Y
A   O   S     E   D   P
S Q U A W K B O X   U S A
K     A   R       T   D
    F O X W O R T H Y
W   I     O     A       S
E R S   D U M B C L U C K
A   H   W       K   N   I
S U N D E C K   S O C K S
E   E   L       G   U   L
L I T T L E B O P E E P
```

SORRY
(Pages 86-87)

```
I B E G Y O U R   S T U B
N   O   E   S     A   A
T O S C A L E   P A P E R
E   U   S   U   A   I   K
A U D I T   P A R D O N
R   I       O   C   L
S U M   B O A R D G A M E
    E   E E L   Y       A
W A S P N E S T   W H I P
I   T   E   O   D   A   F
G O O D F O R   R A N D R
H   R   I   A   A   O   O
T W E E T   N O T H I N G
```

AT'S SOMETHING ELSE
(Pages 88-89)

```
A T T O R N E Y I N L A W
E   U   A   R   N   U   O
R E N E W   M I N I C A M
O   E   D   I   E   I   A
S E R G E A N T S   F U N
O       A   E       E
L A P E L S   I N A R M S
    R       A   O       H
T O O   M I L K S H A K E
U   B   I   D   W   L   B
T W O P A I R   E V I T A
U   N   M   I   A   B   N
S T O P I N N O T H I N G
```

ETHAN ALLEN'S DICTIONARY
(Pages 90-91)

```
F A J I T A   H U M A N E
U   A   B     P   L   Q
S A C R I F I C E   I O U
E   U   R   D   N   B   A
D A Z E D   O D D B A L L
    Z       L       B
I C I C L E   U R B A N E
N   O       I       V
R E N E W A L   S C I F I
U   O   T   A   E   M   L
I H O P E   G E R M A N E
N   N   C   E       G   Y
S H E P H E R D   H E R E
```

ANSWERS

WILD ANIMALS
(Pages 92-93)

```
G E N T L E A S A B A L M
O   O   O   T   D   R   O
U P S E T   A T E D I R T
D   W   S   L   P   Z   L
A G E S A G O   T B O N E
    A     S     N   A   Y
G E T O N E S T O G A
U       E     N           W
L A L A W   A T L A R G E
C   U   B   Z   E   U   N
H A N D O U T   A T B A T
E   A   R   E   V   I   I
S P R I N G C H E C K I N
```

HOW MUCH IS THERE?
(Pages 94-95)

```
  M A S S H Y S T E R I A
A   R   A   E   A   U   S
L O B B Y   L I K E N E W
A   O   S   L   E   W   A
S T R A W B O S S   I N N
K   H   W       L
A R E A O F   G I R D L E
    S     S   S   S     V
N I P   E X P E R T I S E
E   A   P   E   A   S   N
G A N G S T A   E X A M S
E   O   O   R   L   A   O
V O L U M E S W I T C H
```

GNOT IN MY DICTIONARY!
(Pages 96-97)

```
  G N A T T U R N E R
  O   W   P   A   A   M
G R O W O L D   O U T R E
N   S   P   A   M   R   T
A R E N A   T H I N A I R
S   I   E       C   O
H U N G R Y   R A T E D G
V   O   E   L   N
I G N O R E S   A I M T O
L   S   O   C   B   O   M
L O T U S   A S A R U L E
E   O   S   P   M   R
  P H I B E T A G N U
```

FAST FOOD, HASTY READING
(Pages 98-99)

```
Q U A R T E R   B A M B I
T   R   O   I   L   A   S
I N C U R   P O U N D E R
P   H   S   O   E   O   A
  W H O P P E R   N E E
G   A   E       N       L
O R Y   T O N E D E A F
P       O       O
L I M B O   J U N I O R
A   A   L   A   J   N   L
C H I C K E N   U N C L E
E   Z   I   E   A   U   S
S C E N T   T E N D E R S
```

183

ANSWERS

YOU WANNA PIECE O' ME?
(Pages 100-101)

Crossword grid solution:

```
  L O S E Y O U R H E A D
S   R   R   F   A   A   E
C H I N A   F L Y T R A P
U   O   K   N   E A T   O
L E N D A N E A R   S   T
P   X   Y   H   S
T E C H I E   B O T T O M
  R   N E D       A
G U Y   G I V E A H A N D
I   W     E       L   E
Z O O M S I N   F E T I D
M   L   I   S   D   A   O
O F F E R Y O U R A R M
```

NCIS
(Pages 102-103)

Crossword grid solution:

```
W H I S T   B A N A L
S I N C E   I H O P E
J E T H R O G I B B S
      W I N D   U S S
F E T A   C A T
A V A   R E D C A P E
H E T T Y   D U C K Y
D R I V E B Y   A G E
    S S E   H I S S
A W S   E L S E
D A N I E L A R U A H
A W A R D   G O N N A
M A G E S   O D I N G
```

MARTIN SCORSESE MOVIES
(Pages 104-105)

Crossword grid solution:

```
G A L A S   M B A S
L L A M A   A U R A
U S L A W   I R I S
G O O D F E L L A S
    O I L S
L O T   T V I D O L
I M O K   E T A P E
T A X I D R I V E R
T H I N E   N E R O
B A N D I T   S A Y
    L O O T
R A G I N G B U L L
H O M E   S I S S Y
E K E S   U L N A E
A I N T   P L A T S
```

DAVID FINCHER MOVIES
(Pages 106-107)

Crossword grid solution:

```
B U F F   S O C I A L
U B I D   E X A C T A
S E G A   V E R I F Y
H R H   H E Y S
    T H I N E   P C B
P I C O T   D I A R Y
A B L E   K N O T
S A U D I   V O I C E
O R B   F R A N C
    S T U N   R A W
M E G O H M   D O O R
E M B L E M   N O N E
R O S I N Y   A M E N
```

ANSWERS

THREE BY BRADBURY
(Pages 108-109)

Crossword grid solution:

Row 1: GRAB | | SRA | | OGOD
Row 2: RAGU | WAF | LIMA
Row 3: ARID | ABRIDGED
Row 4: DANDELIONWINE
Row 5: YUL | SSE
Row 6: CDI | LOB | ASTER
Row 7: HALLOWEENTREE
Row 8: GULAG | AXE | ALA
Row 9: GIL | PSI
Row 10: DINOSAURTALES
Row 11: SMOOTHIE | MOLE
Row 12: CAAN | TES | BOSS
Row 13: SCHS | ISS | SPAS

THE UNABOMBER
(Pages 110-111)

Crossword grid solution:

Row 1: SAKE | TWOWAY
Row 2: ULAN | HONORE
Row 3: RECT | RMONTH
Row 4: FEZ | TEES
Row 5: YEMEN | STD
Row 6: SINAI | SHERE
Row 7: LASS | OVAL
Row 8: ONKEY | EJECT
Row 9: PSI | EXXON
Row 10: WAFT | THO
Row 11: MIDORI | MEDS
Row 12: SCROLL | META
Row 13: TIEDYE | ENVY

TAKE A HIKE
(Pages 112-113)

Crossword grid solution:

Row 1: BOARD | FRIGID
Row 2: OLLIE | ASSISI
Row 3: NATCHEZTRACE
Row 4: ONSHORE | NHS
Row 5: TRA | GENIE
Row 6: BICENTENNIAL
Row 7: EMIRS | POD
Row 8: AGR | VICUNAS
Row 9: PACIFICCREST
Row 10: AMUSED | HELEN
Row 11: LESSEE | ISLAS

WATERGATE
(Pages 114-115)

Crossword grid solution:

Row 1: JUICE | IBEAM
Row 2: ASTOR | DERMA
Row 3: RESIGNATION
Row 4: ALSO | WERE
Row 5: BODS | NEE
Row 6: UVA | COVERUP
Row 7: LETGO | ENATE
Row 8: BREAKIN | PER
Row 9: TEA | PSST
Row 10: ALOE | GOAT
Row 11: BOBWOODWARD
Row 12: AREAR | INRED
Row 13: BERYL | ESSES

ANSWERS

STEINBECK CLASSICS
(Pages 116-117)

```
V A L E ■ A S P E N
I B A R ■ R O U T E
C A N N E R Y R O W
K N E E L ■ A L I T
■ ■ S B A ■ E L O
E A S T O F E D E N
A L E ■ W O R ■ ■
S T R S ■ N U R S E
T H E R E D P O N Y
O E S T E ■ T W E E
N A T A L ■ S E E S
```

SAME CLUE
(Pages 118-119)

```
Y A M S ■ E A R T H
U N I T ■ S L I W A
M A L E R A B B I T
A T L E E ■ S A N T
■ ■ P G A ■ L G E
T O S S A R I D E R
R P T ■ L M N ■ ■
A T E N ■ O A S E S
D O L L A R B I L L
E U L E R ■ I T O O
S T A R E ■ T E N T
```

MAKING A MURDERER
(Pages 120-121)

```
J O I S T ■ S T E E P
O C C U R ■ H I V E S
S T E V E N A V E R Y
H O E ■ A E R O ■ ■
■ ■ E D G E ■ T N T
B A L L S ■ S T A I R
A B E S ■ ■ A U T O
R E N E W ■ U P S E T
E T S ■ O K L A ■ ■
■ ■ B O O S ■ P O I
B L O O D S T A I N S
F E A R S ■ E X P E L
F E R N Y ■ R E E S E
```

BERNIE MADOFF
(Pages 122-123)

```
A R O M A ■ C A I N E
L O U I S ■ A C C E L
P O N Z I S C H E M E
E S C ■ S A T ■ B E V
S T E F A N I ■ E S E
■ ■ ■ L I E ■ E R I N
■ M R E D ■ A V G S
R E A D ■ S R I ■ ■
E S T ■ P U R L I E U
A S A ■ A L I ■ K A N
L I F E S A V I N G S
M A I L S ■ A D E L E
S H A M E ■ L O W E R
```

ANSWERS

SHUT DOWN
(Pages 124-125)

```
R I F L E   H O S T A   O S S
O N I O N   A R E A S   U K E
B E R I G H T B A C H   T I N
      S A U L   R O T A T E D
L O W   G R O G   B R O O D S
O M E L E T   O N E A L L
C E R E S   M O L L Y   A A A
K N E E   M O N E L   B U R G
E S C   P A P E R   C O N G O
      L O O N E Y   C A N C U N
S H O R T Y   S A H L   H E Y
N E T G A M E   S A L E
A A H   G O N E F I S S I O N
I R E   E R I S A   O S A K A
L T S   S E D E R   N O M S G
```

HASHTAG HUMOR
(Pages 126-127)

```
S C R A P   C L E A T
U H U R A   B R A S C O
B O E R S   R O M P E R
J U R A S S I C P O R K
      Y A W N E R S
P E A   G E E   E I N E
E R A S E   M Y T H S
N O R W   U N E   O L E
      D E A L S T O
L O V E M E F E N D E R
I N A T I E   O S A G E
M E R I T S   R E R A N
P O K E Y   S T A D T
```

JOHN GOTTI
(Pages 128-129)

```
G A T E   D A P P E R
A X E L   H E A R Y E
R E F I   A R G U E D
Y S L   O B I E
    O L D I E   R E B
S Y N O D   S T A L E
C O D A   A C M E
A L O N G   N I K O N
M O N   A P P L E
    S L U R   T E E
M E N T O R   M E A L
O S C A R S   L E S S
B O O T E E   B R E A
```

LIFE IS BUT A DREAM
(Pages 130-131)

```
A G O R A   A C M E S
C A L E B   C H O S E
T R E V I   T A N T E
A N G E L S O F G O D
      L E H R E R
P A T I N A   E D T
S T O N E P I L L O W
A F L   E N E S C O
      L A A L A A
B A R L E Y B R E A D
A R O A R   I N U R E
E L A T E   N E W M E
R O D E O   D R E S S
```

ANSWERS

PALINDROMES
(Pages 132-133)

```
L E V E L ■ E M D A S H
E L I S A ■ V I R I L E
S A V O Y ■ E N A M O R
S T E P O N N O P E T S
■ ■ S V E L T E ■ ■ ■ ■
H E D ■ E R Y ■ R N A S
C E N T R ■ ■ P Y L O N
L E A H ■ A N A ■ E L L
■ ■ ■ U P R O S E ■ ■ ■
A S A N T A A T N A S A
B O R D E R ■ E N I A C
C A M E R A ■ U I N T A
D R Y R O T ■ R O T O R
```

SUMMER CAMPS
(Pages 134-135)

```
H I K E S ■ ■ Z U L U S
C H O S E ■ I R I N A ■
A N D O R ■ P E R I S ■
■ ■ P I L L ■ E V E ■ ■
I V E H A D I T ■ ■ ■ ■
S E R A ■ S N A C K S ■
B R A G A ■ E L L I E ■
N A T U R E ■ L A T E ■
■ ■ S C R E A M E D ■ ■
B O O ■ H I N D ■ ■ ■ ■
O R A T E ■ I E V E R ■
R E F E R ■ A G E N A ■
N O S E Y ■ C A N O E ■
```

BAKER STREET REVISITED
(Pages 136-137)

```
S L A B ■ T H E M E ■ ■
H E L L S ■ B R A V E D
A V I A N ■ A I L I N G
W I T H O U T A C L U E
■ ■ S O R E L Y ■ ■ ■ ■
A F T ■ Z E D ■ O V E R
I R E N E ■ A N I T A ■
M Y N A ■ A N G ■ A C E
■ ■ M O R A L S ■ ■ ■ ■
E N T E R T H E L I O N
A O R T A S ■ A I S L E
T R E A T Y ■ M E L D S
S I E G E ■ ■ R E S T ■
```

BARBERSHOP QUARTET SONGS
(Pages 138-139)

```
A B B E S S ■ T A S K S
L A R V A E ■ H I R E S
S W E E T A D E L I N E
O L D ■ I M A M S ■ ■ ■
■ ■ S N A R E ■ D A B ■
D E N I E R ■ S O D O ■
I D O N T K N O W W H Y
A D D S ■ U B E N D S ■
L Y E ■ P A R S E ■ ■ ■
■ ■ D E D E E ■ B R O ■
U P A L A Z Y R I V E R
S E E I T ■ E V A D N E
P E R I S ■ V E S S E L
```

ANSWERS

LARGE NUMBERS

(Pages 140-141)

```
M E N D S  [ ] S H O R T A
A C E I T    A E I O U Y
D U O D E C I L L I O N
D A N S E U S E S
      T P S    N E V I S
W A R  L A B  A A R E
T R E D E C I L L I O N
W A D E  K O A  O C S
O M A R R    N P R
        B A L D E A G L E
V I G I N T I L L I O N
E N N E A D   E L A N D
R O U S T S   D Y N E S
```

NEOLOGISMS

(Pages 142-143)

```
F L A G   C R U E T S
L A D E   L E S S E E
A T O M   I P E C A C
P E R     A F A R
      K E P I S   M A E
S H A D E   T E A L S
A A B A     S N A P
S A L M I   M A S S Y
S S E   S Y R U P
        B R O S   L U G
B A T E A U   E A S E
S A N S E I   K I E L
C A T T L E   E N D S
```

RIDERS IN THE SKY

(Pages 144-145)

```
D E E R E   A L E R T
A R R A Y   S I N E W
W I N G F D H O R S E
S C O L D S   N I C E
        A R O W   C U T
C H I N O   A C H E S
R A M   P E R L
I R A S   A G E N D A
S A G I T T A R I U S
I R E N E   M I R E S
S E D G E   E C O L E
```

SEEN AT PICNICS

(Pages 146-147)

```
F L A S K   S C A R E
A D L A I   H H O U R
D R I N K C O O L E R
F S T   I A G O
      C D L I   D A L
B R U N E I   D I R E
B A R B E C U E P I T
L I N C   O T E L L O
S D S   A C E S
        B R A N   D S M
I N S E C T S P R A Y
M E R L E   I R O N S
S C A L D   L O P A T
```

ANSWERS

SEEN AT THE GROCERY
(Pages 148-149)

```
D U C K  █  H O N E Y
I K E A  █ W E R E N T
F R E N C H B R E A D
█ █ S U E R S █ █ █ █
█ B A A B A A █ T I P
R O S S █ T I S A N E
P L A S T I C W R A P
M A I T R E █ A O N E
S S R █ A S A N T E █
█ █ L I B E L █ █ █ █
T O M A T O S A U C E
R E D S O X █ K N A R
L O S E R █ █ E A T S
```

AT THE PLAYGROUND
(Pages 150-151)

```
S E E S A W █ D J E D
W A P I T I █ R U D I
A L I S T S █ Y N E Z
█ █ █ S U P E R G █ █
M O P Y █ █ G O L D A
E N L █ M I D T E R M
D E A █ O D O █ G L I
E L Y S I A N █ Y A S
A B H O R █ █ H M O S
█ O N E I D A █ █ █ █
S H U N █ C H I N U P
P O S E █ E A T O N S
A B E T █ S L I D E S
```

CLIP JOINTS
(Pages 152-153)

```
B O A R █ P B S █ M O E
O R L E █ A A H █ E A T
C O M B A S Y O U A R E
A N A I S █ S E S S █ █
█ █ █ R K O █ S A U N A
E Y E T E S T █ R E S █
B U S H W H A C K E R S
B L O █ █ A B A N D O N
S E T U P █ U I E █ █ █
█ █ E R O S █ R A M B O
C U R L U P A N D D Y E
S R I █ N E D █ E S T D
I N C █ D D S █ D E E S
```

COLORFUL PHRASES
(Pages 154-155)

```
R O M P S █ C S P O T
A R E C A █ A T R U E
P U R P L E P R O S E
█ S U P R E M E S █ █
B S A █ T E A S █ █ █
A N N L E E █ S I K H
N A N A S █ E E R I E
S P E W █ A T D A W N
█ █ M A L E █ N I S █
S T E A M E R S █ █ █
P I N K P A N T H E R
A N G E L █ A L O H A
T E R R E █ L O O S E
```

190

ANSWERS

THINGS YOU DO FOR LUCK
(Pages 156-157)

C	H	U	B	B	Y	■	S	T	O	N	E
F	U	T	I	L	E	■	P	H	O	B	E
O	N	A	J	A	G	■	I	R	O	C	S
■	■	■	O	R	O	M	E	O	■	■	■
R	E	D	U	N	D	E	R	W	E	A	R
E	W	R	■	E	S	L	■	E	L	I	O
L	E	A	R	Y	■	P	R	I	M	O	■
I	A	N	A	■	I	B	I	■	S	E	M
C	R	O	S	S	F	I	N	G	E	R	S
■	S	A	S	E	B	O	■	■	■	■	■
C	H	I	L	D	■	R	A	B	B	I	T
D	A	R	E	I	■	C	L	E	A	R	Y
C	L	A	R	E	■	E	L	L	I	E	S

AESOP'S FABLES
(Pages 158-159)

C	A	M	E	L	■	M	O	O	■	A	P	E
A	C	E	L	A	■	O	C	A	■	L	E	A
B	E	L	L	I	N	G	T	H	E	C	A	T
■	■	■	S	N	E	E	■	U	G	H	■	■
O	P	T	■	I	A	N	S	■	G	E	N	E
F	A	R	M	E	R	■	K	I	S	M	E	T
T	R	I	O	■	S	T	I	R	■	Y	E	A
■	■	■	S	I	R	■	E	P	I	C	■	■
T	H	E	L	I	O	N	S	S	H	A	R	E
E	E	C	■	A	W	E	■	E	I	D	E	R
A	N	T	■	L	E	T	■	S	P	A	D	E

WHAT'S IN A NAME
(Pages 160-161)

L	A	P	I	S	■	O	A	R	S	■	S	I	A	M
A	L	A	R	M	■	T	R	A	P	■	U	L	N	A
N	I	C	K	O	F	T	I	M	E	■	P	L	O	T
G	E	T	S	O	R	E	■	P	A	G	E	A	N	T
E	N	S	■	T	E	R	P	■	K	U	R	T	■	■
■	■	■	C	H	A	S	T	I	T	Y	B	E	L	T
A	T	R	I	S	K	■	B	R	O	S	■	A	E	R
B	E	A	D	■	■	P	O	E	■	■	A	S	T	O
I	S	R	■	B	O	C	A	■	P	R	I	E	S	T
T	H	E	F	I	R	S	T	N	O	E	L	■	■	■
■	■	■	B	E	E	B	■	S	A	N	G	■	C	H	A
S	P	I	L	L	I	T	■	S	T	A	B	L	E	S
E	A	R	L	■	S	O	C	C	E	R	M	O	M	S
A	L	D	A	■	O	N	E	A	■	D	O	N	E	E
M	E	S	S	■	N	E	E	R	■	S	C	E	N	T

LOTS OF S'S
(Pages 162-163)

S	E	L	L	O	U	T	■	S	I	R	E	N
E	■	A	■	H	■	U	K	■	A	■	E
E	S	S	A	Y	■	R	A	I	N	B	O	W
Y	■	A	■	E	■	N	■	P	■	B	■	W
A	U	G	U	S	T	A	■	O	U	I	J	A
■	N	■	■	B	■	U	■	V
H	E	A	D	O	F	L	E	T	T	U	C	E
A	■	N	■	I	■	T	■	T
N	U	B	I	A	■	N	O	S	H	O	W	S
G	■	A	R	■	D	■	N	■	P	■	I
M	A	C	H	O	N	E	■	A	M	I	G	O
A	■	K	■	L	■	Y	■	F	■	A	■	U
N	A	S	A	L	■	E	Q	U	I	N	O	X

191

ANSWERS

COCKEYED OPTOMETRIST
(Pages 164-165)

```
T A M P S   F S T O P   T B S
S P A R E   A M O U R   O U I
P R I E S T M O T T O   O T T
      C A M E T O   C O T T A
H O M E M A D E   E L O P E R
U S O P E N   G R A Z E R S
S L I T   S E A M I E R
K O S   A N A G R A M   M I L
    T H R O N G S   A I D E
T A P E R E D   B R U T E S
A Z O R E S   S W E A R S A T
M A T E S   A T E A S E
A L T   T O T R I M P O E T S
L E E   E L M O S   E L L I S
E A R   D E E P S   D E F E R
```

NEGATIVE WORDS
(Pages 166-167)

```
G I S T       U N F I T
O N Y O U     S H A M E
A A R O N     M A R E S
T R I   D I A   R A T
S E A S O N   S A S S
    A N T I P A T H Y
      A N E M O
    D I S G R A C E D
S I G H   I N K P O T
I S U   A L I   O R U
L O A D S   T A C I T
O W N U P   A C H A T
S N A G S   E S N E
```

WORDS FROM OTHER LANGUAGES
(Pages 168-169)

```
K A Y A K   M O P E D
C R E E L   A D O L F
A M A R O   L A D Y L
R A G   N M I   U S A
S T E A D Y   C N E T
    A R T I C H O K E
      A K E E M
    S E R E N A D E S
A T R I   A D R E A M
D E R   B E L   L F O
D R O N E   A M P A S
U N L I T   M O O R S
P O L K A   P A T I O
```

AMERICAN PLAYWRIGHTS
(Pages 170-171)

```
Z I P P Y   T O N K A
E N O L A   R Y A N S
E D W A R D A L B E E
S O S   N E V   S W A
      E E L E D
S A L A D   L E V I N
A G E S     S A M E
M A M E T   S K Y P E
      L A T H S
A B E   B A I   D A B
H O R T O N F O O T E
M A G O O   T A L O N
E S S E S   S T E P S
```